Responding to Violence on Campus

Jan M. Sherrill, *Editor*
Towson State University
Dorothy G. Siegel, *Editor*
Towson State University

NEW DIRECTIONS FOR STUDENT SERVICES
MARGARET J. BARR, *Editor-in-Chief*
Texas Christian University
M. LEE UPCRAFT, *Associate Editor*
Pennsylvania State University

Number 47, Fall 1989

Paperback sourcebooks in
The Jossey-Bass Higher Education Series

Jossey-Bass Inc., Publishers
San Francisco • Oxford

Jan M. Sherrill, Dorothy G. Siegel, (eds.).
Responding to Violence on Campus.
New Directions for Student Services, no. 47.
San Francisco: Jossey-Bass, 1989.

New Directions for Student Services is published quarterly by Jossey-Bass Inc., Publishers (publication number USPS 449-070). Second-class postage paid at San Francisco, California, and at additional mailing offices. POSTMASTER: Send address changes to Jossey-Bass Inc., Publishers, 350 Sansome Street, San Francisco, California 94104.

Editorial correspondence should be sent to the Editor-in-Chief, Margaret J. Barr, Sadler Hall, Texas Christian University, Fort Worth, Texas 76129.

Library of Congress Catalog Card Number LC 85-644751

International Standard Serial Number ISSN 0164-7970

International Standard Book Number ISBN 1-55542-856-8

Cover art by WILLI BAUM

Manufactured in the United States of America. Printed on acid-free paper.

Ordering Information

The paperback sourcebooks listed below are published quarterly and can be ordered either by subscription or single copy.

Subscriptions cost $56.00 per year for institutions, agencies, and libraries. Individuals can subscribe at the special rate of $42.00 per year *if payment is by personal check.* (Note that the full rate of $56.00 applies if payment is by institutional check, even if the subscription is designated for an individual.) Standing orders are accepted.

Single copies are available at $12.95 when payment accompanies order. (California, New Jersey, New York, and Washington, D.C., residents please include appropriate sales tax.) For billed orders, cost per copy is $12.95 plus postage and handling.

Substantial discounts are offered to organizations and individuals wishing to purchase bulk quantities of Jossey-Bass sourcebooks. Please inquire.

Please note that these prices are for the calendar year 1989 and are subject to change without notice. Also, some titles may be out of print and therefore not available for sale.

To ensure correct and prompt delivery, all orders must give either the *name of an individual* or an *official purchase order number.* Please submit your order as follows:

Subscriptions: specify series and year subscription is to begin.
Single Copies: specify sourcebook code (such as, SS1) and first two words of title.

Mail orders to:
Jossey-Bass Inc., Publishers
350 Sansome Street
San Francisco, California 94104

New Directions for Student Services Series
Margaret J. Barr, *Editor-in-Chief;* M. Lee Upcraft, *Associate Editor*

SS1 *Evaluating Program Effectiveness,* Gary R. Hanson
SS2 *Training Competent Staff,* Ursula Delworth
SS3 *Reducing the Dropout Rate,* Lee Noel

SS4 *Applying New Developmental Findings,* Lee Knefelkamp, Carole Widick, Clyde A. Parker
SS5 *Consulting on Campus,* M. Kathryn Hamilton, Charles J. Meade
SS6 *Utilizing Futures Research,* Frederick R. Brodzinski
SS7 *Establishing Effective Programs,* Margaret J. Barr, Lou Ann Keating
SS8 *Redesigning Campus Environments,* Lois Huebner
SS9 *Applying Management Techniques,* Cecelia H. Foxley
SS10 *Serving Handicapped Students,* Hazel Z. Sprandel, Marlin R. Schmidt
SS11 *Providing Student Services for the Adult Learner,* Arthur Shriberg
SS12 *Responding to Changes in Financial Aid Programs,* Shirley F. Binder
SS13 *Increasing the Educational Role of Residence Halls,* Gregory S. Blimling, John H. Schuh
SS14 *Facilitating Students' Career Development,* Vincent A. Harren, M. Harry Daniels, Jacqueline N. Buch
SS15 *Education for Student Development,* Jane Fried
SS16 *Understanding Today's Students,* David DeCoster, Phyllis Mable
SS17 *Developmental Approaches to Academic Advising,* Roger B. Winston, Jr., Steven C. Ender, Theodore K. Miller
SS18 *Helping the Learning-Disabled Student,* Marlin R. Schmidt, Hazel Z. Sprandel
SS19 *Mentoring-Transcript Systems for Promoting Student Growth,* Robert D. Brown, David A. DeCoster
SS20 *Measuring Student Development,* Gary R. Hanson
SS21 *Helping Students Manage Stress,* Elizabeth M. Altmaier
SS22 *Student Affairs and the Law,* Margaret J. Barr
SS23 *Understanding Student Affairs Organizations,* George D. Kuh
SS24 *Commuter Students: Enhancing Their Educational Experiences,* Sylvia S. Stewart
SS25 *Orienting Students to College,* M. Lee Upcraft
SS26 *Enhancing Student Development with Computers,* Cynthia S. Johnson, K Richard Pyle
SS27 *Students as Paraprofessional Staff,* Steven C. Ender, Roger B. Winston, Jr.
SS28 *Rethinking Services for College Athletes,* Arthur Shriberg, Frederick R. Brodzinski
SS29 *Facilitating the Development of Women,* Nancy J. Evans
SS30 *Applied Ethics in Student Services,* Harry J. Canon, Robert D. Brown
SS31 *Coping with Death on Campus,* Ellen S. Zinner
SS32 *Working with the Parents of College Students,* Robert D. Cohen
SS33 *Enhancing Relationships with the Student Press,* John H. Schuh
SS34 *Developing Campus Recreation and Wellness Programs,* Fred Leafgren
SS35 *Alcohol and the College Student,* Thomas G. Goodale
SS36 *Guiding the Development of Foreign Students,* K Richard Pyle
SS37 *Expanding Opportunities for Professional Education,* Leila V. Moore, Robert B. Young
SS38 *Responding to the Needs of Today's Minority Students,* Doris J. Wright
SS39 *Enhancing Campus Judicial Systems,* Robert Caruso, Will W. Travelstead
SS40 *Fraternities and Sororities on the Contemporary College Campus,* Roger B. Winston, Jr., William R. Nettles III, John H. Opper, Jr.
SS41 *Managing Student Affairs Effectively,* M. Lee Upcraft, Margaret J. Barr
SS42 *Changing Roles for Men on Campus,* Ronald J. May, Murray Scher
SS43 *Performance Appraisal as a Tool for Staff Development,* Robert D. Brown

SS44 *Empowering Women: Leadership Development Strategies on Campus,* Mary Ann Danowitz Sagaria
SS45 *Dealing with the Behavioral and Psychological Problems of Students,* Ursula Delworth
SS46 *Religion on Campus,* John Butler

Contents

Editors' Notes

While college campuses have a history of student activism, which is sometimes blighted by isolated acts of violence, campuses have also always had the tranquillity associated with intellectual pursuit. Part of the reason for this tranquillity may be that the age of majority used to be twenty-one and colleges and universities, acting in loco parentis, tended to prolong childhood. Violations of good conduct were often viewed simply as "playground misbehavior." Any egregious behavior was handled by civil authorities.

Now, however, what was once termed "high jinks" may constitute criminal behavior. Much of the violence that college administrators and faculty believed only happened to others, outside the walls of the campus community, happens today in dormitories, student unions, and college classrooms. Sexual assault on women seems to be on the increase, and this is not simply because students have become more aware of date rape and report it with greater frequency. What is perhaps most troubling is the climate for violence that may exist on many college campuses. We must be concerned not only about the number of women who are attacked but also about the growing tendency among students to resort to violence as a means of resolving conflict.

Violence on college campuses is not only, as was once thought, imported by nonstudents. Results from the Towson State University Campus Violence Surveys indicate that most violence on college campuses is student-to-student violence and that only a portion of the violence that actually occurs is reported. Yet the myth of the safe campus endures. The FBI's *Uniform Crime Report,* to which 10 to 15 percent of campuses subscribe, does not begin to tell the whole story. Student perceptions of violence, when compared to the statistics in the *Uniform Crime Report,* suggest that a college community, particularly one that is largely residential, might become inured to a certain amount of violence and thus allow it to go unreported.

Violence done to members of those groups that have historically been disenfranchised—such as gays and racial and ethnic minorities—continues to be unreported. The AIDS epidemic has given a new intensity to violent homophobia, and unfortunately, antisemitism and racism live on college campuses just as they do in most American communities. Vandalism seems to occur with greater frequency than in the past. Anonymous graffiti have given way to major property destruction, including damage to elevators, bathroom fixtures, permanent art collections, and campus library holdings.

The intention of this sourcebook is twofold: first, to enlarge what is sometimes only a marginal discussion of the problem and, second, to work toward prevention of violence, decreasing university liability while enhancing staff and student safety. This volume will be successful if it augments efforts already under way to end campus violence and if it generates concern and discussion within individual college communities. Self-examination is crucial in beginning to address the issue of violence.

In the first chapter, Michael Clay Smith looks at the origins of campus violence and tells us that the problem is not a new one. He also provides a possible explanation for why the myth of the safe campus persists. Chapter Two, by Marion Cockey, Jan M. Sherrill, and Robert B. Cave II, analyzes the Towson State University surveys of chief student affairs officers, directors of residence, and campus police or safety directors as to their official reports and their own perceptions of violence on college campuses.

Ralph L. V. Rickgarn discusses violence in residence halls in Chapter Three. He makes clear that such incidents may be termed domestic violence, for they resemble closely, both in form and in effect on the victims, such violence in society at large.

Mary L. Roark, in Chapter Four, focuses on sexual violence on campus and emphasizes means of combatting such abuse and of educating for prevention. Then, in Chapter Five, Nancy Greene Cerio compares the various approaches taken by those in college communities who counsel victims and perpetrators of campus violence. Cerio also discusses the role of campus police or security personnel as first-on-the-scene interventionists.

Chapter Six is Christine Steiner's analysis of current issues of campus administrators' rights and liabilities. She emphasizes, through discussion of a specific case, the role of campus police and security, preventive security measures, and issues of recordkeeping and confidentiality.

Jan M. Sherrill, in Chapter Seven, discusses models for addressing campus violence. Different types of responses, from the use of local civil authority to that of on-campus disciplinary proceedings, are given consideration. Factors such as school size and type of campus (residential versus commuter) also influence an institution's response to violence.

Chapter Eight concludes the volume with a listing of additional sources of information, for this work is just beginning and many areas need further exploration.

We are indeed grateful to our authors not only for their fine chapters but also for their commitment to this work. We wish to thank especially Gordon Chapman, editor of *Response to the Victimization of Women and Children,* for his tireless and gracious help; Leonard Goldberg, vice-president of student affairs at the University of Richmond for his original interest and support of the Campus Violence Survey; Mary Lee Farlow, director of residence at Towson State University; the Campus Violence Committee, who advised and worried; Deborah Shaller for editorial advice; and the Student Services Division at Towson State University for its patience, vigor, and wisdom. Finally, special thanks go to Dianne Thompson and Patricia Holmes, who saw the manuscript through from thought to page.

Jan M. Sherrill
Dorothy G. Siegel
Editors

Jan M. Sherrill is assistant vice-president for student services at Towson State University and director of the Center for the Study and Prevention of Campus Violence.

Dorothy G. Siegel is vice-president for student services at Towson State University and executive director of the Center for the Study and Prevention of Campus Violence.

While campus crime is now disturbing the entire nation, its long and sometimes violent history shows that it is not a completely new problem.

The Ancestry of Campus Violence

Michael Clay Smith

America's college and university campuses present increasingly evident anomalies: by and large they are physically attractive, inviting places that may, in reality, be quite dangerous, and they are places where openness of thought is fostered but physical access and movement frequently must be fettered.

The deceptively safe appearance of many campuses, together with a conventional attitude that sees colleges as peaceful havens set apart from the "real world," no doubt exacerbates the problems of campus crime and violence. Getting younger students, and even adult employees and visitors, to take self-protection seriously is a problem everywhere. Many persons become victims simply because they are not on guard.

In fact, campuses have never been without crime and violence, although the nature and extent of the campus crime seen today clearly have never existed before. Further, it is interesting to discover that the common notion of a campus as a sort of sanctuary from the troubles of the world had its beginnings in medieval "town versus gown" disputes.

Origins of the Campus as Sanctuary

The medieval universities were developed by and for the Catholic church, and originally they were operated as ecclesiastical communities

J. M. Sherrill and D. G. Siegel (eds.). *Responding to Violence on Campus.*
New Directions for Student Services, no. 47. San Francisco: Jossey-Bass, Fall 1989.

similar to monasteries. But, as it became evident that educational power leads directly to political and economic power, the secular authorities began to want some of the action, and a power struggle developed between the princes and the bishops over control of the universities. In addition, an enmity sometimes emerged between the townsfolk whose communities surrounded the universities and the scholars, with their boisterous festivities and haughtiness that accompanied their literacy and privileged status. Occasionally this enmity erupted into violence, such as the bloody rioting at Oxford that began on the Feast of Saint Scholastica in 1354. It raged for three days, leaving the university pillaged and many dead, among them two chaplains who were flayed alive (Schachner, 1938).

As a result of these problems, the various crowns began granting special independent legal status to the universities so that they could operate without excessive secular interference. This special status typically included the right of students and faculty to be tried in ecclesiastical or university courts, rather than the town's courts, for any charged offense (Smith, 1988). Colleges around the world inherited something of this tradition of independence from governmental authority, and out of it came the notion of the campus as a sanctuary.

The dearth of earlier cases involving higher education in the nation's appellate court reports and the absence of regulatory legislation at either federal or state levels could imply that there were few legal requirements affecting the administration of American institutions of higher education until as late as the 1960s. Unquestionably this was true regarding the common-law principle of in loco parentis, under which educational authorities acted in place of and with all the authority of a student's parents. Certainly for its first several centuries, America's higher education establishment "tended to think of itself as removed from and perhaps above the world of law and lawyers" and was left to "regulate itself through reliance on tradition and consensual agreement" (Kaplin, 1985, p. 3).

Early Campus Crime in America

This attitude helps to account for the lack of reported court cases involving crime or violence at our colleges and universities of yesteryear, but it certainly does not mean they never happened. Rather, student conduct that might have constituted a criminal offense in the outside world was handled, in the eighteenth and nineteenth centuries, by the faculty, which sometimes served as a "high court of justice, whose judicial duties were only second to its teaching business" (Coulter, 1951, p. 62). By the twentieth century, such matters were usually handled by the dean of students, who sat as the prosecutor, jury, and court of highest appeal. Nonstudents, who nowadays are a significant source of crime on many campuses, had little opportunity for campus crime in earlier times, since most campuses were small, most students were full time, and intruders on a campus were obvious.

Still, college histories from earlier decades of American history include occasional notorious crimes, such as the conviction in 1850 of a Harvard medical professor for the murder of another physician. The victim's body was never found, and the prosecution contended that the professor had dismembered him and disposed of the remains in the college's medical laboratory (*Commonwealth* v. *Webster,* 1850).

High expectations of personal conduct marked American college life prior to the twentieth century, local customs notwithstanding. Even though dueling was not an uncommon method of settling disputes over honor in the old South, when one University of Mississippi student wounded another with a pistol in a dispute over a lady at a university ball just before the Civil War, the faculty expelled the wounded student and advised the other to "withdraw" from the university for an indefinite period of time (Cabiniss, 1971; Lloyd, 1979).

In the first half of the nineteenth century, many college students were dissatisfied with rigorous discipline and spartan living conditions, which led to occasional unrest and even violence. At the University of Virginia, rebellious students rioted at various times during the 1820s to 1840s, killing a professor and, on one occasion, bringing the local sheriff and armed constables onto the campus to restore order. Half the Princeton student body was suspended after a violent rebellion in 1807, and, in another riot several years later, Princeton's president, the Reverend Dr. Ashbel Green, reported the firing of a pistol at a tutor's door, the breaking of "a great deal" of glass, and an attempt to burn campus outbuildings (Brubacher and Rudy, 1976).

At Yale in 1841, students bested New Haven firefighters in a street fight and destroyed their equipment. In 1854, a fight between New Haven residents and Yale students led to the death of a local bartender, and, four years later, the second "Firemen's Riot" ended when a student shot and killed a firefighter. Historian William H. Prescott lost an eye during a brawl in the Harvard Commons while he was a student around 1820, and one Harvard tutor of the period incurred a lifelong limp as a result of his confrontation with student rioters. On another occasion, the college expelled more than half the senior class on the eve of commencement (Brubacher and Rudy, 1976).

Education historians Brubacher and Rudy explain the violence of early American campus life as a reflection of the social fabric of the exuberant young nation, in which there was an "inner conflict between an overrepressive, Calvinistic morality and a frontier pattern of heavy drinking and brutal fighting" (p. 55). There is little information concerning campus crime, violence, or other misconduct in the period between the Civil War and World War II. This absence of data can be reasonably interpreted to mean that crime and violence were not significant problems.

Modern History of Campus Crime

The American higher education scene changed fundamentally after World War II. A confluence of factors, including the radically heightened need for education and credentialing in the postwar world, the financial accessibility of college for returning veterans provided by the GI Bill of Rights, and the arrival of the "baby boom" generation in the 1960s, caused an exponential growth in the numbers of colleges and the numbers of people attending them. By the 1970s, the higher learning scene was much more diverse, encompassing part-time students, commuter campuses, cooperative programs with business and industry, and enrichment curricula for ethnic minorities and for returning adults, all heretofore nontraditional students. As a far larger and more mainstream portion of the population entered the campuses, the problems of the parent culture were certain to follow (Smith, 1988).

Widespread violence and lawbreaking, however, entered modern campus life with two clearly identifiable social phenomena of the 1960s: the civil rights movement and the Vietnam War protests. It is paradoxical that commonplace violence seems to have been ushered into campus life by such laudable social movements. Still, by the early 1970s, thousands of students and other demonstrators had faced criminal charges growing from campus marches, sit-ins, draft-card burnings, and even riots in support of political ideology and social change (Smith, 1988).

In 1968, for the first time in American history, mass felony indictments were returned against students as a result of campus unrest. The charges resulted from the student occupation of the administration building at San Fernando Valley State College, where the president and other college personnel had been held captive for several hours. The Los Angeles County grand jury indicted the twenty-four students on charges of kidnapping and false imprisonment, and all but one were convicted. Reflecting the social transformation he was witnessing, the presiding judge ruled that "college campuses are not privileged sanctuaries where disruptive, violent, felonious acts go unpunished" (Blackwell, 1974, p. 3).

The violence of the period reached a lethal peak in 1970, when members of the National Guard fired into a crowd of students at Kent State University, killing four and wounding nine. A few days later, police officers fired into a dormitory at Jackson State College (now University) killing two and wounding twelve (President's Commission on Campus Unrest, 1970).

Incidents of campus crime continued to increase through the 1970s and early 1980s, reaching a plateau that has held steady through recent years. The FBI's *Uniform Crime Report* regularly records several thousand crimes of personal violence (homicide, forcible rape or robbery, and aggravated assault) and in excess of 100,000 serious property crimes (burglaries and serious thefts) on America's college and university campuses each year (U.S. Department of Justice, 1987).

These figures are much smaller than the actual total. Less than one fifth of the nation's higher education institutions report statistics for the *Uniform Crime Report,* which is based on voluntary self-reporting by institutions, and the campus statistics do not include off-campus incidents involving students, even though many institutions rely heavily on private housing, especially for upper-division students. In addition, because institutions want to project positive public images, there is reason to suspect that some colleges' reports are understated. It is revealing that a recent poll by Gallup for *Newsweek* magazine ("Worrying About Crime," 1986) disclosed that 38 percent of the nation's college students reported worrying about crime on or near their campuses "a great deal" or "a fair amount."

Civil Liability: The Legacy of Campus Crime

In this decade, the courts have formulated new legal theories of liability under tort law in order to assist victims of campus crime and, it is hoped, to spur campus administrators to ameliorate risks. The courts are moving rapidly and boldly to require institutions to protect their students and employees from the ravages of crime, and the institution—as well as the individual administrator—that fails to provide such protection may be liable to victims in large civil suits for money damages.

Until recently, colleges were not liable to persons who happened to become the victims of crime on campus. As recently as 1974, the California Supreme Court refused to impose liability on the University of California, Santa Barbara, in a suit brought on behalf of two young men who were beaten, one fatally, while sleeping overnight on a beach owned by the school. The assailants were never identified. Even though there was some history of crime in the area, the court applied the old doctrine that the owner of real estate had a duty to warn only of physical dangers in the real estate itself and that an owner was not liable for crimes committed on the property by third persons (*Hayes* v. *State,* 1974).

Now this legal principle is being supplanted by one that imposes liability in money damages where a history of crime in the area has made it "foreseeable" that trouble might occur but the institution did not take adequate protective steps or warn potential victims—especially students—of the danger. The supreme courts of at least five states have endorsed the foreseeability doctrine in connection with campus crime cases in *Miller* v. *State of New York* (1984), *Mullins* v. *Pine Manor College* (1983), *Jesik* v. *Maricopa County Community College District* (1980), and *Tarasoff* v. *Board of Regents* (1976).

These and other related cases have identified three general categories of legal duty for colleges and universities with regard to campus violence: a duty to warn potential victims of danger, a duty to screen student applicants for dangerous persons, and a duty to provide adequate protective measures.

A landmark decision involving the duty to warn of danger was *Peterson* v. *San Francisco Community College District* (1984), a decision of the California Supreme Court, which held that Kathleen Peterson could maintain a damage suit against the institution for injuries received in an attempted rape in a college parking lot, because the college had been aware of previous assaults there but had not warned students.

A related case, also from California, held that campus administrators have a duty to be candid and forthcoming when inquiries are made about campus safety. *Duarte* v. *State* (1979) was brought by the mother of a female student who was sexually assaulted and murdered by a sailor who broke into her dormitory at one of the campuses of California State University. Before enrolling her daughter at the school, the mother had asked school officials about crime and safety, and she had visited the dormitory. She testified that she had relied on the representations that the dormitory was a safe place and on its appearance of safety and security when she decided to let her daughter live there. The school did not give warning of prior crimes in the area, and, the California Court of Appeals found, the representations that the dormitory was safe were made by university officials "with presumed superior knowledge" about the actual crime history. The court said that such representations could support a suit for fraud and deceit.

A duty to screen college applicants for dangerous persons has been the basis of one major legal case, *Eiseman* v. *State of New York* (1987), which made its way through the entire New York court system. It grew out of an experimental program for disadvantaged persons at the State University of New York College at Buffalo. One such student, whose application revealed he would attend as a paroled felon, was invited to a party at the off-campus apartment of another student. There, the parolee went on a bloody spree of rape and murder that left two students dead and a nonstudent companion repeatedly stabbed. Later it was found that the parolee's history included stabbing and shooting, armed robbery, seventeen years of heroin abuse, and many other violent psychotic episodes. Parole officials had known of this history, but the college had made no effort to learn details of the man's background even though his admission documents revealed that he was a prisoner when he applied and that he had been incarcerated once before.

The trial court awarded more than $360,000 to the family of one of the murder victims, and the award was upheld by the intermediate courts, but New York's highest court ultimately overturned the verdict. The high court noted that prison and parole officials had been found free of negligence in the release of the prisoner and said that the college should not be held "to a higher duty than society's experts in making such predictions" (p. 616). The court also stated that the college had no heightened duty to screen the applicant, even though administrators knew they were dealing with an ex-offender, and likewise no duty to restrict such an admittee's activities with other students.

While this singular decision has left colleges, at least in New York, without any duty to screen applicants, it is not certain that other courts would reach the same legal conclusion when dealing with applicants who are known criminals and whose violent propensities might be readily foreseeable. In addition, the duty to warn fellow students of the potential threat, balanced against the convict's right to privacy and Buckley amendment concerns, remains to be explored further in subsequent cases.

Once a college or university is on notice of the likelihood of criminal harm because of a history of criminal incidents and the risk is thus foreseeable, the institution has not only a duty to warn but also a duty to protect. This may take the form of adequate fences, lighting, locks, telephones, and security guards, as well as designing or adapting the campus physical plant so that hiding places for assailants are minimized, and dormitories, libraries, cafeterias, and parking lots are safely accessible to students. In addition, academic scheduling may need modifications so that classes are not offered in remote places at dangerous times.

Three cases are illustrative of the need to protect students through appropriate security measures once the foreseeability of crime has been established. In *Miller* v. *State of New York* (1984), a nineteen-year-old female student was confronted in the laundry room of her residence hall at six one morning by a man wielding a large butcher knife. She was blindfolded and prodded out of the room, then out of the basement through an unlocked outer door, back into another unlocked entrance to the dormitory, and upstairs to a third-floor room where she was raped twice at knifepoint under the threat of mutilation or death if she made any noise. Finally, she was led out to a parking lot where the assailant fled. He was never identified.

In her suit against the college, the student showed that, prior to the attack, strangers were not uncommon in dormitory hallways and that there had been reports to campus security of men being in the women's bathroom. The student herself had twice complained to the dormitory supervisors about nonresidents loitering in the dormitory. The school newspaper had published accounts of numerous crimes in the dormitories, such as armed robbery, burglaries, criminal trespass, and rape by a nonstudent. Nonetheless, all ten dormitory doors were admittedly kept unlocked at all hours. New York's highest court said that the college was in essence a landlord and owed students a duty to maintain "minimal security measures," which it had not done in Miller's case. Ultimately, an award of $400,000 to the student was upheld.

A similar decision finding foreseeability, based on less of a campus criminal history than the Miller case but with a greater proximity to a dangerous urban area, was rendered by the Massachusetts Supreme Court in *Mullins* v. *Pine Manor College* (1983). Lisa Mullins was awakened in her dormitory room in the early morning hours by a male intruder who placed a pillowcase over her head and marched her out of the dormitory and across the campus into the refectory building, then back outside, then into the refectory again where he raped her. He fled and was never identified. The whole episode lasted sixty to ninety minutes, and the pair was outside for at least twenty minutes.

While the only criminal history on campus included a burglary in the dormitory one year before and a male intruder into Mullins's dormitory commons the previous night, the campus was located near bus and subway lines that led directly to Boston. The evidence showed that dormitory locking systems were rudimentary and doors could easily be opened with credit cards or knives, that fence gates around the campus were not locked and the fences themselves could easily be scaled, and that, although two guards were on duty at night, no system ensured that the guards were performing patrols—an important issue since the incident lasted so long without detection. The court left standing the jury's verdict of $175,000 against the college's vice-president for operations and a $20,000 verdict against the college itself.

Adequacy of police protection was the central issue in an Arizona case, *Jesik* v. *Maricopa Community College District* (1980). Peter Jesik was registering for fall semester classes in the college's gymnasium when an argument erupted with another student. The other student told Jesik he was going home to get a gun and would come back to kill Jesik. Jesik then told a college security guard and received assurances of help and protection. Later, when the other student returned, Jesik again appealed to the guard and was assured of protection. The guard talked to the student who had made the threat but did not look into his briefcase. When the guard departed, apparently satisfied, the student pulled a handgun from the briefcase and killed Jesik. The slain student's family sued, and the Arizona Supreme Court affirmed a judgment against the college.

Although the court did not specifically discuss the "foreseeability" doctrine in connection with the plaintiffs' claim, the court adopted a corollary principle based on a specific, enunciated threat. Because of the specific death threat, the court held, the college should have taken bolder protective action because of its duty to exercise reasonable care to protect its students.

In one recent case, the California Court of Appeals declined to extend a college's duty of protection to off-campus sites even though they immediately adjoin the campus itself and are necessarily utilized by those attending the institution. In *Donnell* v. *California Western School of Law* (1988), a law student was stabbed by an unknown assailant as he walked toward his parked car after studying one night in the law library. The law school building occupies one city block in San Diego, and the attack occurred on a public sidewalk along the west side of the building.

The school provided no parking for its students. Even though there had been previous criminal activity in the area, the building had no exterior lights on its west side, and no security guards were provided to patrol the area. Nonetheless, the court held that, because the school did not own the sidewalk, it could exercise no control over it, and thus it did not owe a duty to protect its students on the sidewalk. Issues of duty owed to students off campus have not been adequately explored in the existing cases, and future decisions may clarify the duty of colleges and universities, especially as to warning of danger.

The preceding landmark cases have significantly changed the law and are likewise changing many campus administrative practices. Express or implied in the decisions is the realization that college and university administrators traditionally have had little motivation to acknowledge the extent of campus crime by imposing conspicuous security measures or warning potential victims. With the declining enrollments that followed the "baby boom" glut of students, administrators have understandably concentrated on good public relations for their institutions, unfortunately sometimes at the cost of responding to the campus crime risk and of protecting potential victims.

Of course, not all institutions and administrators can be tarred with this brush. Many colleges and universities have always maintained exemplary security programs and have promptly taken all measures necessary for the protection of students, employees, and guests. Colleges and universities have won and continue to win many of the crime-based liability suits brought against them, either because the particular crime had not been foreseeable or because the administrators had adequately responded to foreseeable crime with reasonable protection and warnings before the criminal incident (Smith, 1988).

In other cases where foreseeability has not been established, plaintiffs have lost. In *Relyea* v. *State* (1980), a damage suit was brought over the deaths of two Florida Atlantic University students who were abducted and murdered when they returned to their car after an evening class. Although the heirs of the young women alleged the university had a general duty to protect them, the court found that, where there had been no other violent crime on the campus and there was no other reason to foresee danger, the institution had no duty to anticipate danger from a third party.

The Florida courts have made clear, however, that, where colleges, universities, and even high schools are on notice of prior crime to the extent that they should foresee danger, they have a duty to take reasonable precautions to protect the students, and they will be liable if they do not.

As in the *Relyea* case, murder was involved in a North Carolina case, *Brown* v. *North Carolina Wesleyan College* (1981), in which a court found that the attack had not been foreseeable and therefore dismissed the suit. The suit was brought in 1980 after a cheerleader was abducted from a basketball game on the campus and later was raped and murdered. Examining the evidence, the court found that the only other significant crimes on campus that had preceded the abduction were a break-in at the college business office a dozen years earlier, vandalism of vending machines five years earlier, and one report of an attempted rape two years earlier. These were insufficient for the college to foresee the abduction and therefore no duty to the student was breached, the North Carolina Court of Appeals ruled. Similar holdings came in cases involving a Southern University coed who was shot in the lobby of her dormitory by a nonstudent; a woman who was injured in an auto crash that followed a dormitory drinking party at California Polytechnic State University, San Luis Obispo; and a student who was stabbed during a racial disturbance at a Glassboro State College basketball game.

Conclusion

Campus crime and violence have long histories. Nonetheless, in the current crime plague, America's campuses face a unique threat to their health and the fulfillment of their missions. The response of colleges and universities to crime is of singular consequence. It has been said that our institutions of higher education are the matrix of our culture, since they form the people who become our culture's leaders. This being so, the response of the colleges and universities to the manifestation of crime in the midst of campus life has special significance for the future of our society.

References

Blackwell, T. E. *The College Law Digest, 1935–1970.* Washington, D.C.: National Association of College and University Attorneys, 1974.

Brown v. *North Carolina Wesleyan College,* 309 S.E.2d 701 (N.C. 1981).

Brubacher, J. S., and Rudy, W. *Higher Education in Transition.* (3rd ed.) New York: Harper & Row, 1976.

Cabiniss, A. *The University of Mississippi: Its First Hundred Years.* Hattiesburg: University and College Press of Mississippi, 1971.

Commonwealth v. *Webster,* 59 Mass. (5 Cush.) 295, 52 Am. Dec. 711 (1850).

Coulter, E. M. *College Life in the Old South.* Athens: University of Georgia Press, 1951.

Donnell v. *California Western School of Law,* 246 Cal. Rptr. 199 (Cal. App. 4 Dist. 1988).

Duarte v. *State,* 88 Cal. App. 3d 473, 151 Cal. Rptr. 727 (1979).

Eiseman v. *State of New York,* 518 N.Y.S. 2d 608, 511 N.E. 2d 1128 (1987).

Hayes v. *State,* 521 P.2d 855 (Cal. 1974).

Jesik v. *Maricopa County Community College District,* 611 P.2d 547 (Ariz. 1980).

Kaplin, W. A. *The Law of Higher Education: A Comprehensive Guide to Legal Implications of Administrative Decision Making.* (2nd ed.) San Francisco: Jossey-Bass, 1985.

Lloyd, J. B. *The University of Mississippi: The Formative Years, 1848–1906.* John Davis Williams Library Archives and Special Collections, University of Mississippi, 1979.

Miller v. *State of New York,* 467 N.E. 2d 493 (N.Y. 1984); as for damages, see 487 N.Y.S. 2d 115 (1985).

Mullins v. *Pine Manor College,* 449 N.E. 2d 331 (Mass. 1983).

Peterson v. *San Francisco Community College District,* 685 P.2d 1193 (Cal. 1984).

Report of the President's Commission on Campus Unrest. Washington, D.C.: U.S. Government Printing Office, 1970.

Relyea v. *State,* 385 So.2d 1378 (Fla. 1980).

Schachner, N. *The Medieval Universities.* New York: Barnes, 1938.

Smith, M. C. *Coping with Crime on Campus.* New York: American Council on Education and Macmillan, 1988.

Tarasoff v. *Board of Regents,* 551 P.2d 334 (Cal. 1976).

U.S. Department of Justice, Federal Bureau of Investigation. *Uniform Crime Report.* Washington, D.C.: U.S. Government Printing Office, 1987.

"Worrying About Crime: A Student Poll." *Newsweek on Campus,* February 1986, p. 10.

Michael Clay Smith is legal counsel, and holds a joint appointment as associate professor in the departments of criminal justice and educational leadership and research at the University of Southern Mississippi.

Towson State University's two national surveys are analyzed. Concerns and inadequacies of the FBI's Uniform Crime Report *are discussed.*

Towson State University's Research on Campus Violence

Marion Cockey, Jan M. Sherrill, Robert B. Cave II

Fifteen years ago, the student population on most campuses seemed a relatively sedate group. Any behavior requiring more than a perfunctory reprimand either became the subject of some ongoing counseling or, if the behavior was criminal, was handled by civil authorities. Because violent criminal behavior was extremely rare, this policy was effective. Ten years ago, however, an incident occurred on the Towson State University campus that caused real change in university policy. A student who had become drunk at a party assaulted a resident assistant who had been called by complaining residents to break up the party. Dorothy Siegel, vice-president for student services at the time, felt that an institution had an obligation to support and protect its staff. The assailant was suspended from the university.

The climate for tolerance of such student misbehavior was changing even at that time. Judges in civil courts had already begun to express displeasure at having to take actions that they thought were more rightly the responsibility of individual institutions. As higher education became less a privilege and more a necessity, students increased their expectations and, at the same time, took on more individual responsibility (Smith, 1988).

J. M. Sherrill and D. G. Siegel (eds.). *Responding to Violence on Campus.*
New Directions for Student Services, no. 47. San Francisco: Jossey-Bass, Fall 1989.

In the last few years, informal discussion among administrative personnel and among faculty at regional conferences pointed out that many schools were experiencing violent behavior among their students. No one seemed completely clear as to whether this problem was growing or whether dealing with these problems simply seemed to take a disproportionate amount of time and energy. One thing was sure: with heightened consumer awareness, the reexamination of the roles of women and men in our society, and the litigious climate of the nation in general, violent behavior on campus, regardless of its nature and frequency, runs counter to the academic missions of our institutions and is detrimental to the kind of world that higher education has always hoped to foster. In order to ameliorate the problem, however, college administrators first needed to assess it.

At Towson State, we realized that students knew more about acts of violence on our campus than we did. We undertook, in the spring of 1985, to survey our own students for their perceptions of the amount of violence on our campus (see Appendix I). We found that, indeed, many more students said they had either been victims of some form of violence or knew of a greater number of violent incidents than our official reports indicated. It also became apparent that some of our own offices on campus—the Residence Department, for example—had a different perception of the amount of violence that occurred on campus than did other offices such as the campus police.

With the help of the National Association of Student Personnel Administrators (NASPA), Region II, we undertook to survey the NASPA-affiliated schools in our region as a pilot project. We asked for recorded statistics from police or security departments, deans of students, judicial affairs offices, residence departments, and student union offices on each campus.

Interest in the survey, as indicated by the respondents to the regional survey, was keen. At their suggestion, we modified the number of offices surveyed to three: deans of students, police or safety departments, and residence departments. Over the past two years, we have conducted two national surveys and will continue to conduct yearly surveys to note trends. Towson, along with NASPA II and the American College Personnel Association's (ACPA) Commission One Task Force on Violence and Victimization on Campus, has also hosted two national conferences on the subject of campus violence, and this year the Center for the Study and Prevention of Campus Violence has been established at the university.

Official Statistics

The official statistics most often utilized to assess the amount of violence on college campuses are found in the *Uniform Crime Report (UCR),* which is issued annually by the Federal Bureau of Investigation. Each *UCR* summarizes data sent voluntarily by police agencies across the United States. It reports the Crime Index: eight crimes considered serious by nature or frequency. The index crimes are murder, rape, robbery, aggravated assault, burglary, larceny theft, motor vehicle theft, and arson. Data are gathered on twenty-three additional crimes, such as simple assault, gambling, and vandalism. The *UCR* is called uniform because each offense has a definition specified by the FBI that may or may not agree with each local jurisdiction's definition. For example, purse snatching falls in the category of larceny theft in the *UCR,* but in many jurisdictions it constitutes robbery since there is usually a confrontation between the purse snatcher and the victim. Only crimes recorded become labeled as "known to police"; this means that a crime can be reported to the police but not recorded by them. It is also important to note that, because reporting to the FBI is voluntary, estimates are that only 10 to 15 percent of college campuses actually turn over statistics.

The issue of reporting and recording may be especially significant to the study of campus violence because of the myriad methods of handling data on campuses. Residence directors may not report incidents that are handled internally by residence staff. The same may be true of student union and recreational directors on campus. A nonsworn police agency may hand over all cases to the local sworn police agency, which then would not differentiate between the campus statistics and the jurisdiction's statistics. On the other hand, the campus agency may only turn over those cases it cannot handle on its own. It is very difficult to determine the differences among procedures of reporting and recording that exist on all of the campuses that send data to the *UCR.*

Another issue of concern to college administrators is the fact that the schools listed in the *UCR* change from year to year because reporting is voluntary. This makes it very difficult to compare statistics over time or across campuses. For example, in 1985, the University of Maryland at College Park was labeled the most violent campus, although its official reported rate was approximately 170 incidents per 100,000 persons, about one fifth of the crime rate of the surrounding community and much lower than the national average for typical neighborhoods.

Thus, the many problems inherent in the official statistics include: their voluntary nature; the fact that only some crimes are included; the fact that local jurisdictions must fit their data to *UCR* definitions; and the fact that the index crimes, which are often taken to represent the "state of crime," reflect mostly street crimes of fear—violent offenses that reflect approximately 10 percent of the total crimes known to police in a given year. Each offense has its own "likelihood of report" rate.

Official statistics are manipulated both intentionally and unintentionally. Crime statistics are subject to nonreporting, nonrecording, over-reporting, and concealment. Some of the general factors that may affect the accuracy are political considerations, accuracy of data keeping, policy on which crimes to record, personnel needs, research requirements, equipment shortages, and a host of other issues that may affect the day-to-day operations and decisions of a police department. As far as concealment is concerned, anecdotal evidence suggests that departments may keep two sets of records—one for internal use and one for "public consumption."

The 1987 *UCR* for colleges and universities, which reports on crime in 1986, includes no listing at all for eight states (Alaska, Delaware, Hawaii, Idaho, Montana, New Hampshire, South Dakota, and Vermont). Reports of violent crime are missing from sixty-two of the schools that did respond. A total of 399 schools reported their data for the 1987 *UCR*. This represents about a 10 percent response rate from the estimated 3,500 colleges and universities in the nation.

The following warning is given in the *UCR:* "The reader is, therefore, cautioned against comparing statistical data of individual reporting units from cities, counties, states, or colleges and universities on the basis of their population coverage or student enrollment" (U.S. Department of Justice, 1987, p. v). In addition: "Caution should be exercised in making any intercampus comparisons or ranking schools, as university/college crime statistics are affected by a variety of factors. These include: demographic characteristics of the surrounding community, ratio of male to female students, number of on-campus residents, accessibility of outside visitors, size of enrollment, etc." (p. 118).

In spite of the various warnings and limitations, we realize that, since we have only one source for official statistics on campus crime, we must use the *UCR*. We know that unofficial statistics almost always reveal greater incidence of crime than the official statistics. We still, however, need a baseline of sorts, and the official statistics provide that baseline.

Unofficial Statistics

Unofficial statistics are those gathered by studies of victims of crime, self-report methods, and by observation; generally speaking, they are those developed by academicians or consulting groups, not police. The picture presented by the unofficial statistics is far different from that of the *UCR*. The issues that make official statistics difficult to compare with the unofficial include: the definitions of crime, which may not be shared by the respondents; confusion about the time frame in which crime occurred, falsehoods or inaccuracies in people's reports; lack of questions about where people were victimized; data not requested on all types of crimes; inclusion of only victims over the age of twelve; and the inability to verify reports with official statistics. The results of victimization studies suggest that the volume of crime is far greater than anything suggested in official statistics.

One thing that we have learned from victimization studies is that teenagers are the least likely of any age category to report victimization. In addition, consensual crimes, or what used to be called victimless crimes, are not likely to be reported. These crimes include drug-related offenses. Also, each community has its own threshold for criminal activity, and a college community is no different. What one campus may consider to be "college pranks" may in fact be criminal behavior. Yet another reason for nonreporting is that the situation may be embarrassing for the victim; this is especially true in cases of date rape.

Limitations of the Towson State Surveys

Several methodological notes are necessary. Our surveys did not specify *aggravated* assault, which refers to bodily harm, but rather asked how many physical assaults were reported. The expectation, therefore, is that our number might be much higher overall since all levels of assault are included.

Because we sought answers from three separate offices on any given campus and because, in order to protect anonymity, we did not identify how many individuals at the same college or university responded to the questionnaire, some data may be skewed. If one school with very high victimization had all three offices respond, the overall outcome will reflect that.

Another concern is the inevitable question of to what extent are those responding different from those who fail to respond? One could argue that the more serious the violence problem at a school, the more likely the participation since the school would be interested in any effort to gather information and investigate possible remediation. But one might also argue that, if there is significant violence, schools may not participate in order to maintain the image of a safe campus. Campuses' self-perceptions may be the major factor affecting our surveys' response rates.

Finally, the fact that these surveys strictly use the self-reporting method, asking for perceptions as well as facts, may account for the variance in the amount of violence reported by different offices—residence directors versus chief student affairs officers, for example. That variance, however, may indicate the largest problem in which all campuses share: lack of uniform knowledge.

The reports of Towson's national surveys follow. The response rates, as noted, vary and are another obvious limitation of our data. Despite this fact, the surveys have been highly successful in encouraging open discussion of problems of campus violence, since assessment of the problem is the first major step toward eliminating the problem.

1986 National Survey

This survey was distributed nationwide to 1,100 colleges and universities (NASPA member institutions) in April of 1986 (see Appendix II).

The student affairs, police/security, and residence departments of these institutions were each provided with a separate copy of the survey and asked to supply the requested information from their 1985-86 records. Of the 3,300 copies distributed, 764 (roughly 24 percent) were completed and returned. Of those returned, 42 percent were from student affairs, 31 percent were from police/security, and 26 percent were from residence. The information given below has been compiled from the responses of the student affairs officers and is based on response means. (For greater detail, see the "1986 Preliminary Report," available on request from the Center for the Study and Prevention of Campus Violence, Towson State University, Towson, Maryland 21204.)

The average respondent institution:

- Has between 1,001 and 5,000 students
- Is located in the southern or midwestern region of the United States
- Is located in an urban or rural setting
- Is coeducational
- Has a population that can be described as 80.3 percent white, 10.3 percent black, 4.0 percent Hispanic, 2.2 percent Asian, 2.3 percent Native American
- Has a resident population of 35.2 percent.

Half of the respondents were public and half were private institutions.

Sexual Assault. During the academic year 1985-86, the average campus experienced 4.0 sexual assaults (excluding rapes) and 1.6 rapes.

Half (48.6 percent) of the respondents perceived date rape to be a significant part of the sexual assaults that occur on their campuses; half (48.2 percent) did not. Those who did report that 44.6 percent of on-campus sexual assaults are date rape.

Of the on-campus reported incidents of sexual assault, 19.2 percent resulted in criminal prosecution, 39.4 percent resulted in university penalty, 5.4 percent involved the use of alcohol, and 9.3 percent involved controlled substance or drug use. One third (34.1 percent) of the on-campus sexual assaults were reported to campus police or security. Between two thirds and three fourths (71.4 percent) of these incidents were perpetrated by students.

One fifth (19.0 percent) of the respondents reported an increase in sexual assaults from 1984-85 to 1985-86.

Physical Assault. During the academic year 1985-86, the average campus experienced 10.2 physical assaults.

Of the on-campus reported incidents of physical assault, 5.5 percent involved the use of deadly weapons, 57.8 percent resulted in a university penalty, 16.0 percent resulted in criminal prosecution, 53.9 percent involved the use of alcohol, and 14.0 percent involved controlled substance or drug use. Almost two thirds (62.9 percent) of the on-campus physical assaults were reported to campus police or security. Almost three fourths (71.8 percent) of the on-campus physical assaults were perpetrated by students.

One fourth (24.7 percent) of the respondents reported an increase in physical assaults from 1984–85 to 1985–86.

Vandalism. Of the on-campus reported acts of vandalism, 53.4 percent involved the defacing and destruction of property, 45.5 percent resulted in university penalty, 7.7 percent resulted in criminal charges or prosecution, 48.2 percent involved the use of alcohol, and 6.9 percent involved controlled substance or drug use. Nearly two thirds (63.3 percent) of on-campus incidents of vandalism were reported to campus police or security. Three fourths (75.1 percent) of these incidents were perpetrated by students.

Nearly one third (29.6 percent) of the respondents reported an increase in vandalism from 1984–85 to 1985–86.

General Information. Fifty-three percent of the respondents have campus security that is affiliated with state or local police; 44.1 percent do not.

Of the respondents, 93.1 percent have provisions for immediate suspension of a student who constitutes a real or perceived danger to others on campus, while 4.1 percent have no such provisions; 89.8 percent of the respondents feel they could exercise this authority, and 7.3 percent feel that they could not.

Seventy-six percent of the respondents feel that the majority of violent incidents on their campuses are reported; 21.2 percent feel that the majority are not reported. Most respondents (90.7 percent) are confident that their institutions can handle problems of violence; 6.4 percent are not.

1987 National Survey

This survey was distributed nationwide to 1,100 colleges and universities (NASPA member institutions) in April of 1987. The student affairs, police/security, and residence departments of these institutions were each provided with a separate copy of the survey and asked to supply the requested information from their 1986–87 records. Of the 3,300 copies distributed, 917 were completed and returned. Of those returned, 40 percent were from student affairs, 30 percent were from police/security, and 30 percent were from residence. The information given below has been compiled from the responses of the student affairs officers and is based on response means. (For greater detail, see the "1987 Preliminary Report," available on request from the Center for the Study and Prevention of Campus Violence, Towson State University, at the address provided in the previous section.)

The average respondent institution:

- Has between 3,000 and 5,000 students

- Is located in the northeastern, southeastern, or midwestern region of the United States
- Is located in an urban setting
- Is coeducational
- Is public
- Has a population that can be described as predominantly (90.4 percent) white
- Has a resident population of 28.4 percent.

Sexual Assault. During the academic year 1986–87, the average campus experienced 2.2 sexual assaults (excluding rapes) and 2.1 rapes. Of these sexual assaults, 23 percent were date rape.

Of the on-campus reported incidents of sexual assault, 17 percent resulted in criminal prosecution, 26 percent resulted in university penalty, 32 percent involved the use of alcohol, and 12 percent involved controlled substance or drug use. One third (31 percent) of the on-campus sexual assaults were reported to campus police or security. Three fourths (75 percent) of these incidents were perpetrated by students. One tenth (9.7 percent) of the respondents reported an increase in sexual assaults from 1985–86 to 1986–87, 61.9 percent reported no increase, and 26.9 percent did not know.

Physical Assault. During the academic year 1986–87, the average campus experienced 8.6 physical assaults.

Of the on-campus reported incidents of physical assault, 11 percent involved the use of deadly weapons, 44 percent resulted in a university penalty, 27 percent resulted in criminal prosecution, 40 percent involved the use of alcohol, and 13 percent involved controlled substance or drug use. One half (49 percent) of the on-campus physical assaults were reported to campus police or security. More than three fourths (79 percent) of the on-campus physical assaults were perpetrated by students.

Almost one fifth (18.3 percent) of the respondents reported an increase in physical assaults from 1985–86 to 1986–87, 60.8 percent reported no increase, and 16.7 percent did not know.

Vandalism. Of the on-campus reported acts of vandalism, 56 percent involved the defacing and destruction of property, 46 percent resulted in university penalty, 15 percent resulted in criminal charges or prosecution, 52 percent involved the use of alcohol, and 16 percent involved controlled substance or drug use. More than one half (57 percent) of on-campus incidents of vandalism were reported to campus police/security. More than three fourths (79 percent) of these incidents were perpetrated by students.

One fourth (26.4 percent) of the respondents reported an increase in vandalism from 1985–86 to 1986–87, 57.5 percent reported no increase, and 15.8 percent did not know.

General Information. Forty-nine percent of the respondents have campus security that is affiliated with state or local police; 44 percent do not.

Of the respondents, 94.1 percent have provisions for immediate suspension of a student who constitutes a real or perceived danger to others on the campus, while 4 percent have no such provisions; 85 percent of the respondents feel that they could exercise this authority, and 12 percent feel that they could not.

Seventy-six percent of the respondents feel that the majority of violent incidents on their campuses are reported; 17 percent feel that the majority are not reported; 7 percent do not know. Between two thirds and three fourths (71 percent) of the respondents are confident that their institutions can handle problems of violence; 23 percent are not; 5 percent do not know.

A comparison of the 1987 survey to the 1986 survey reveals that sexual assault is down, as is date rape; future surveys will determine whether this significant decrease represents a trend. For the time being, any amount of decrease is noteworthy, and a significant decrease is a very hopeful sign. Also hopeful is the fact that only 10 percent of respondents in 1987 felt that sexual assault is on the increase compared to nearly 20 percent in 1986.

Physical assault also appears to be on the decline, and fewer believed that the number of physical assaults is increasing. Finally, colleges and universities seem to be reacting more strongly to all physical assaults on their campuses, for both criminal prosecution and institutional penalties resulting from incidents of physical assault increased from 1986 to 1987.

Conclusions and Recommendations

The extent and nature of campus violence have been made difficult to ascertain by a number of factors. FBI estimates published in the *UCR* are collected on a voluntary basis. Statistics gathered by local police jurisdictions and reported to the FBI do not always separate statistics for institutions from statistics for the communities in which the institutions reside, and only a portion of the total number of postsecondary academic institutions regularly report incidents either to local police jurisdictions or to the FBI. In addition, victims who are college students do not always report incidents and offenses or file complaints. More important, college administrators do not always consider incidents to be actionable or prosecute them in a way that would recognize them as "reported offenses." Moreover, the reporting procedures of academic institutions have been found to be flawed.

The problems of violence are not reported with any regularity either on the national and state levels or on individual campuses. In general observations solicited in the survey, respondents indicated that they are often torn between the bad publicity that violent incidents create and the need to provide an accurate picture of campus conditions. Lawsuits stemming from claims of safe or secure campuses are increasing, however, and administrators are under pressure to find ways to avoid them.

Colleges and universities cannot prevent all criminal incidents from occurring, but they have a duty to act responsibly in terms of security. Students and faculty do not often comply with such security measures as locking rooms and not walking alone on unlighted paths. On the other hand, decisions in lawsuits are holding the colleges responsible for unsafe conditions. Those of us who live or work on a campus must realize that we too have a duty to care and to take responsibility for ourselves and our actions. The Towson State Surveys begin to provide information that may support specific policy changes on campuses. Much more analysis needs to be done; perhaps this chapter will be the impetus for future research.

At this point in our own studies, we can safely conclude that there is a different level of knowledge about violence among various administrators and the police. We have learned that students seem to feel safe despite having been threatened or harassed. We also know that at least some students are armed. Finally, there is a tremendous difference in the likelihood of criminal prosecution versus college penalty, depending probably on campus policy and the perceived seriousness of the offense.

What is sorely needed is a uniform method of reporting, record keeping, and analyzing violence and crime on college campuses. Also needed is what the subsequent chapters of this sourcebook begin to provide: discussion and evaluation of the past and present posture of higher education in relation to campus crime and violence.

The most important implication of the Towson surveys is the mandate to college and university administrators to design and implement prevention plans, safety and security designs, and consciousness-raising activities. A working partnership is needed to help us fulfill our obligations to our own community, for if we do not take on this responsibility ourselves, government may do so for us.

References

Smith, M. C. *Coping with Crime on Campus.* New York: American Council on Education and Macmillan, 1988.

U.S. Department of Justice, Federal Bureau of Investigation. *Uniform Crime Report.* Washington, D.C.: U.S. Government Printing Office, 1987.

Marion Cockey is the corrections coordinator, Department of Sociology, Towson State University.

Jan M. Sherrill is assistant vice-president for student services at Towson State University and director of the Center for the Study and Prevention of Campus Violence.

Robert B. Cave II is associate director of the Center for the Study and Prevention of Campus Violence.

Violence in residence halls can be termed campus domestic violence; it resembles off-campus domestic violence both in its forms and the effects it has on victims.

Violence in Residence Halls: Campus Domestic Violence

Ralph L. V. Rickgarn

There seems to be a myth that the campuses of academic institutions are places where only the highest endeavors of the human mind and spirit exist and the coarseness, vulgarity, and violence of the "outside world" cannot intrude. In other words, it is taken for granted that the campus is a sanctuary where violent acts do not occur. This naive assumption is maintained by campus residents in spite of their actual experiences with theft, harassment, and physical and sexual assault. Yet, on every campus, residents of halls leave their doors open or unlocked while "just down the hall for a minute," assuming that no one in the hall would steal anything. Residents permit total strangers to pass through locked security doors and move about the residence hall's floors without challenge. Caution and a sense of healthy skepticism seem "foreign" in a place where residents assume that the only things that may happen are a few harmless pranks. And there is denial and ingenuous shock when some act of violence takes place in the hall.

But clearly violence in residence halls is not new. While it may be ignored or denied, violence has existed since the beginning of residential units on the campuses of this country. Cowley (1934), in his history of student housing, discussed various incidents of violence that were directed against residence hall staff. Campus violence, however, was not a popular

J. M. Sherrill and D. G. Siegel (eds.). *Responding to Violence on Campus.*
New Directions for Student Services, no. 47. San Francisco: Jossey-Bass, Fall 1989.

topic then (any more than it is now), as administrators did not want reports of misconduct to damage the reputations of their institutions or to create negative impressions among prospective students and parents. So, for many years after Cowley's work, little was written about violence on campus. Part of this may have been due to protectionism and the lack of acknowledgment of various forms of violence against women and minorities that characterized a lengthy period of our history. But it is more likely that the issues were either ignored or denied to avoid any potential embarrassment to the institution. The issues were raised again by Kirkpatrick and Kanin (1957) with their study of male sexual aggression on campus, and in the past ten years there has been an ever-increasing volume of literature and a better understanding of the frequency and intensity of various forms of violence on campus and within residence halls.

The model of violence in residence halls as campus domestic violence comes from two concepts. The first is that violence is a violation of the individual's personal space and/or property. This violence includes physical (injury of person or destruction of property), psychological (threats and intimidation), or both. The second concept is that residence halls are domiciles where relationships of varying levels of intimacy are formed and consummated. These relationships range from friendships to dating and courtship to some relationships that closely resemble those of married couples. Consequently, both predomestic and domestic relationships occur in residence halls. Given the number of different patterns of dating and courtship relationships that exist in residence halls, relationship violence becomes very possible. It appears that the extent of relationship violence in residence halls closely approximates that of the "outside world," and it follows similar patterns. Relationships become abusive and, often aided by the influence of alcohol or other chemical substances, the violence escalates to levels of abuse and injury that neither party would have believed possible. Puig (1984) noted that predomestic strife is a growing concern for college counseling services, since most college communities have had no program to create an awareness of the nature of relationship violence. There is sometimes an awareness of the monetary costs of repair and restoration of damaged or destroyed items but none of the devastating psychological costs to individuals and to the residential community as a result of this violence.

In this chapter, various types of violence against residents and staff will be examined, including physical assault and verbal abuse, sexual harassment, courtship and dating violence, and sexual assault. The ramifications of this violence will be examined, focusing on the possibility that the victim may become a double victim—that is, in some instances, violence against an individual may precipitate the idea or the act of suicide, the ultimate personal violence by an individual against herself or himself.

Verbal Abuse or Harassment and Physical Assault of Staff

Residence staff share the conviction that they can make a contribution to the lives of students, and they value their interactions with the men and women who live in the halls. Most of these interactions are very positive and provide affirmation for their roles in the hall. Indeed, these positive experiences normally outweigh any abuse or harassment, and staff effectively cope with these adverse circumstances. However, when resident assistants (RAs) are victims of abuse or harassment, they may feel responsible; they may believe that residents would not engage in such behaviors if the RAs were adequately doing their job. This belief results in feelings of personal failure and loneliness. Consequently, college administrators need to be aware of adverse actions that can hurt staff morale and result in less effective performance, and they need to support staff who are victimized.

Staff victimization is not a new phenomenon. Cowley (1934) provided a number of specific instances of verbal abuse and harassment as well as physical assaults on individuals who were employed to enforce the rules of college residence. In the intervening fifty-plus years, however, little was written about violent acts on campuses until recently. And, on the campus, these actions by offensive residents were more likely to be discussed and lamented at staff meetings than to be presented to a judicial board.

Residents, often relying on a code of silence or collaboration among members of a floor or house, may enjoy engaging in harassing acts against staff members without realizing the havoc they may cause. Other residents engage in actions consciously intended to hinder the resident assistants' or other residents' activities. They may engage in vendettas against RAs whom they regard as "getting them in trouble" for taking some form of disciplinary measure against them as a result of their past inappropriate behaviors. Alcoholic beverages are often involved as residents who are under the influence are less inhibited, become more aggressive, and are thus more likely to be involved in harassment.

RAs tend to shrug off actions against them as "coming with the territory." Residents decide that it isn't worth the trouble to file a report because they don't want to "get anybody in trouble," are intimidated by some individual or individuals or by the situation, or simply wish to remain anonymous, but this precludes any resolution of the problem through judicial or other disciplinary actions. How pervasive these harassing actions are remains largely unknown, but there are some studies that offer perspective on the extent of the problem.

Schuh and Shipton (1983) found that 50 percent of the RAs (n = 163) surveyed on one campus had encountered obscenities as a major form of verbal abuse, with minority RAs more often the victims of racial slurs and female RAs victims of sexual slurs. Damage threats were reported more often in all-male halls, with malicious pranks and damage being the most common forms of abuse. However, of the sixty-four incidents reported in the survey, only two were reported by RAs for judicial action. These instances involved actual physical abuse such as attack with a weapon, threatening touching, and sexual abuse.

Durant, Marston, and Eisenhandler (1986) conducted a nationwide survey involving 5,902 RAs and 1,847 RA supervisors from 284 colleges and universities. The researchers found that the most common forms of harassment experienced by RAs were harassing language, facial expressions, inconvenient pranks, intentional embarrassment, harassing gestures, harassing graffiti, offensive jokes, and harassing phone calls. Of the responding RAs, 84 percent had experienced these incidents at least once and 34 percent as often as daily. In addition, 23 percent had experienced damage to personal property, 18 percent had experienced physical threats and violence, 12 percent had experienced inappropriate sexual touching, 2 percent had been attacked with a weapon or object, and 1 percent had encountered physical sexual abuse. The RAs reported that alcohol or drugs were involved in 81.4 percent of these incidents.

While it has often been assumed that male RAs were more subject to harassment than female RAs, this was not substantiated by this study. In fact, 44 percent of the female RAs experienced sexist harassment and 19 percent experienced sexual harassment, compared to 13 percent and 8 percent of the male RAs, respectively. The percentages of male and female RAs who experienced general, racial or ethnic, religious, or gay or lesbian harassment did not display any substantial differences between the sexes.

RAs responded to these incidents through formal procedures in about 10 percent of the incidents and utilized informal procedures for 33 percent of the incidents. Most often an RA's first choice of action (where possible) was to confront the abuser face to face; the second choice was to ignore the incident or seek advice from other RAs, supervisors, or fellow residents. Almost half of the RAs state that they felt victimized by what had occurred.

From the information gathered in these two studies, RA harassment is clearly a negative factor for staff in residence halls. In fact, these actions may be more pervasive than reported since the subjective perception by RAs of what constitutes harassment, their perceived ability to manage a situation, and their own value systems will vary significantly. The study by Durant, Marston, and Eisenhandler (1986) demonstrated that there was a significant difference between RA and supervisor perceptions of the seriousness of incidents. Supervisors tended to view a greater number of the reported incidents as serious than the RAs did. This may mean that supervisors are not aware of the vast number of incidents that RAs do not perceive as serious and consequently do not report (harassing incidents that are seen as "part of the job"). Or supervisors, from years of experience, may view these incidents as being more serious. Regardless, there appears to be a growing sense from both RAs and housing administrators that these actions may be increasing and that they constitute deterrents to the RA selection process as more and more prospective RA applicants refuse to apply for positions where they will be subjected to these abuses. More important, such incidents undermine the RA's role in fostering student development, a function that should be the most attractive part of the RA position.

Sexual Harassment of Staff

An often overlooked and sometimes very subtle form of violence against individuals is sexual harassment. This may take the form of subtle gestures, remarks, or innuendos, or it may involve actual physical actions such as patting, pinching, and other forms of inappropriate sexual touching (which may, in fact, constitute sexual assault). Residents, particularly males, often find these actions harmless and view them as the normal "give-and-take" of residential life. Unfortunately, the "boys will be boys" attitude may become the standard frame of reference of both men and women residing in dormitories. There are instances, however, when sexual aggressiveness leads to more violent behaviors, including rape.

Durant, Marston, and Eisenhandler (1986) noted that 12.4 percent of the RAs surveyed reported that they had been the object of inappropriate sexual touching. Schuh and Shipton (1983) reported that sexual slurs were encountered by 16 percent of the male and 51 percent of the female RAs. While only 15 percent of the RAs in all-male halls reported such activity, 31 percent of the RAs in coed halls and 53 percent of the RAs in all-female halls reported these actions. The RAs reported a mean incidence of 4.9 times per year with a range of 1 to 40 incidents. Anyone who has worked in residence halls can certainly cite any number of incidents. These incidents again are often assumed to be "fun" and are not taken seriously, as there are important differences in perceptions of what constitutes sexual harassment. One of the women responding to the study by Durant, Marston, and Eisenhandler (1986) stated: "Because most supervisors are males, harassment can and is easily taken as a joke instead of a violation of rights. Sometimes it can be very difficult to be taken seriously" (p. 27).

These incidents *are* serious, however, and they have an insidious effect on the RA and on the quality of residential life, undermining the positive student development model. Individuals who have to exist in a milieu where sexual harassment appears to be condoned are impacted both socially and emotionally. The results may include an erosion or loss of self-esteem and self-confidence, a feeling of responsibility for the situation, a fear that they will be victimized in the same way as they have seen others victimized, and a fear of violence. In all instances, there is a distraction from the positive potential of the residential and collegiate learning environments, and it may even result in a student making a decision to leave the residential community to avoid this victimization.

Colleges and universities often have sexual harassment policies, but residence staff (much less the residents themselves) seem not to be aware of their rights and responsibilities. Lack of awareness of what constitutes sexual harassment may still be the most serious block to controlling this insidious form of interpersonal violence.

Courtship and Dating Violence

The clearest parallel to domestic violence that exists in the residential setting is that of courtship and dating violence. This cycle of violence follows the typical pattern of a relationship whose problems escalate to the point where one individual (most often the male) engages in some type of emotional or physical battering behavior. After a "cooling-off" period, the batterer returns and promises never to engage in this behavior again. This is followed by the typical "honeymoon" period, which is followed by another escalation of emotions resulting in a battering, and the cycle resumes. Unfortunately, the violence often increases with each cycle. Wetzel and Ross (1983) offer profiles of men who batter and women who have been battered that fit the profiles of individuals who are involved in courtship and dating violence as seen in residences. Residence hall staff should become aware of these profiles to aid in the identification of potential or real problem individuals, and they should develop programs that will enable residents to identify these issues for themselves.

The incidence of courtship violence was first reported by Makepeace (1981). He found that one in five students had a direct personal experience of courtship violence and that a majority of the students knew other students who had been victims. In 82 percent of these incidents, alcohol usage was involved. Bogal-Allbritten and Allbritten (1985) have engaged in the most direct study of the incidence of courtship violence in residence halls. The majority of the students who responded (61 percent) knew of another student who had been involved in courtship violence, and 19 percent acknowledged that they had had at least one personal experience, ranging from threats of bodily harm to slapping, punching, being struck with an object, being assaulted with a weapon, or being choked. These studies indicated that 62 percent of the victims had ended the relationship with the assaulter, 27 percent were continuing the relationship, and 11 percent thought the relationship had become closed "although not necessarily as a result of the violence" (p. 203). While victims had usually not been drinking (17 percent were under the influence), it was reported that 48 percent of the assailants had been drinking.

The responses in this study indicate that the problem of courtship violence in residence halls is well known to residents and that such violence appears to go largely unreported; this parallels off-campus domestic violence, since the incidence of student-reported violence is similar to the incidence of marital violence in other studies. When fellow residents fail to intercede or report the behavior to staff, the residence hall environment appears to condone these actions, and the implicit message may be that this behavior is, in fact, acceptable. Such, acceptance may lead to the impression that this is "normal" behavior and may result in further instances of such acts.

Sexual Assault

Acquaintance or date rape is one of the most violent actions that takes place in residence halls. And, since there are only two parties involved, it is also probably the most underreported major violence. The perpetrator is not about to reveal the act for fear of the possible consequences, and there is some evidence that more assaults might take place if the perpetrator believed the act would not be discovered. The victim is also not likely to report the act for fear of being labeled or of finding that no one will believe what has happened. Most often it is the male that is the perpetrator and the female the victim. However, there are instances of male same-sex sexual assaults that have taken place in residence halls; these are rarely reported since there is a common fear that there will be homosexual implications. The victim is unlikely to understand that the issue is power, not sex.

Koss, Gidycz, and Wisniewski (1987) found that 13 to 25 percent of the women in a national study reported experiencing rape, and 4.6 to 26 percent of the men reported perpetration. Using those reported experiences that met the FBI definition of rape, this study found rates for women that were ten to fifteen times higher than those of the National Crime Survey (NCS) for women ages sixteen to twenty-four. According to Koss, Gidycz, and Wisniewski, "at least among students in higher education, it must be concluded that official surveys such as the NCS fail to describe the full extent of sexual victimization" (p. 168).

As residence halls develop programs to create an awareness of what constitutes sexual assault, more and more reporting of sexual assault in the form of date rape should be forthcoming. Until recently, there was little discussion of this form of sexual assault; when individuals did acknowledge the act, it was "assumed" that this was not sexual assault but rather a part of the "dating game." This is clear from statements made by female victims, such as "No one would believe me because we have been dating for a while and friends do not rape" or "You don't get raped in your dorm room by another resident. That's not the way it happens!" And male perpetrators have attempted to deny any assault by claiming "No doesn't mean no! She wanted it!" or "There wasn't any fighting or anything like that; it was just sex between two people, one who wanted it and one who pretended she didn't as part of the 'act'."

While there are infrequent stranger rapes in dormitories, the predominant sexual assault is acquaintance or date rape, and residence programs need to address this issue specifically.

Ramifications of Violence

From the preceding it is clear that violence in residence halls often goes unreported. Consequently, no disciplinary or legal action can be taken against the perpetrator, and the incident remains unresolved. For the victim, an unresolved violent act can create potentially devastating psychological problems. The victim becomes a victim a second time.

Victimization is a highly traumatic experience in which the victim experiences some degree of loss of personal control. This sense of powerlessness can lead to maladaptive responses to the stress. One of the most tragic results of being a victim of violence is that the victim may do violence to himself or herself. A victim may move through a continuum in which the violent act precipitates depression and feelings of hopelessness. When these feelings are followed by the victim's belief that his or her life is out of control, the individual may engage in suicidal thoughts or actions.

Stark (1985) reported that 44 percent of the sexually assaulted women who were interviewed had seriously thought of suicide, and 19 percent had actually attempted it. Of those who had experienced attempted rape, 19.1 percent had seriously considered suicide, and 8.9 percent had attempted it. There is no way to determine how many women who have been sexually assaulted have committed suicide as a result.

Walker (1984) reported that battered women often resolve their negative feelings about being battered through self-destructive tendencies. For instance, 36 percent of the women in her study had threatened to commit suicide. She reported that 50 percent of the batterers also threatened to commit suicide. The effects of negative self-esteem and other factors are present in both parties and can result in suicidal and homicidal threats.

From these studies and other information it is clear that individuals who are victims are also at high risk for self-destructive behaviors; thus, violence in residence halls has ramifications beyond the original event.

Concepts for Prevention

Understanding the magnitude and significance of violent behaviors on campus and clarifying an institution's philosophy, policies, and procedures with regard to on-campus violent behavior are the first steps in dealing with this problem. An honest awareness of and assessment of violent activity in resident halls and a rejection of denial that such activity exists are essential second steps. Third steps are the giving of permission to report and discuss violent activities accurately and the provision of services for those individuals who are victims.

While there is a temptation to list here campus programs that provide these essentials, it is possibly more helpful to outline the essential components from which any institution can develop a model of response for their residential life program. Roark (1987) suggests a multifaceted approach that includes efforts in three prevention categories: primary, secondary, and tertiary. Primary prevention involves actions that are taken before an incident occurs. For example:

1. Evaluate physical environments to determine what exists on the campus that may create dangerous situations (such as darkened areas on the campus grounds or within buildings), and eliminate these problem areas.

2. Train staff so that they understand the various forms that violence can take, the current probability and extent of violence on the campus, and what they are expected to do when they encounter violent actions. Roark (1987) lists a number of training programs, including values development, assertiveness, and self-esteem. Staff can then transmit this understanding to student residents and begin the development of the most powerful deterrent to campus violence—residential communities that hold any type of violence to be unacceptable.

3. Develop programs and workshops that discuss the nature and causes of violence and attitude formation. And, while much intellectual debate, critical inquiry (the soul of good education), and respectful disagreement may be fostered through programming by residents and staff, the central theme must be stated clearly and repeatedly: violence is unacceptable and perpetrators will face the consequences of their actions.

These actions must be cooperative ventures among various offices: residential life; public safety; parking; counseling; judicial affairs; minority affairs; and other pertinent departments. The involvement of student government is essential so that students understand the issues, the problems, and their own power enabling them to build positive community norms and procedures. Students need to feel that "we're all in this together" rather than believing that it is someone else's job to do the protecting.

Secondary prevention includes efforts to deal with problems already in existence. The major factors are awareness, education, and the establishment and effective implementation of clear policies and procedures. Residential communities will have diverse approaches to attaining these goals. Perceptions and language must change so that violent actions are not dismissed as "just a little scuffle" or "just a lover's quarrel," since this is the beginning of permission for, and acceptance of, violence. Instead, staff and students need to define violence accurately and to state that it will not be tolerated. Policies and procedures that are supported at the highest administrative levels need to be established. The following excerpt from the University of Minnesota's residence hall regulations (University of Minnesota Housing Services, 1988) is an example of this type of policy:

> Behavior involving violations of any of the following regulations which could endanger the safety or well-being of other residents or the residence hall (e.g., tampering with mechanical or fire alarm/safety systems, disorderly conduct, weapons) could result in your immediate eviction from the residence hall . . . :
>
> You are guilty of disorderly conduct if you do any of the following in a public or private place, knowing, or having reasonable grounds to know, that it will or will tend to alarm, anger, or disturb others or provoke an assault or breach of peace:
>
> (a) Engage in brawling, fighting, or prank activities;
> (b) Disturb an assembly or meeting, not unlawful in its character;
> (c) Use offensive, obscene, or abusive language, or engage in conduct that would reasonably tend to arouse alarm, anger, or resentment in others; or
> (d) Threaten, sexually harass, or endanger the health, safety, or welfare of a member of the university community [pp. 16–17].

Such policies and procedures need to be disseminated to all students and have consistent implementation through student conduct codes.

Tertiary prevention involves direct services for victims. These include crisis and medical services, possible protection, establishment of a clear report of the facts of the incident for possible adjudication (criminal and/or within the institution), and posttrauma counseling and support. Victims need this climate of support in order to manage their own fears and confusions, particularly their feelings of "it must have been my fault" or "no one will believe me." These services should also be made available to friends of the victim, as they need similar assistance during this traumatic period. These actions establish a climate within the residential community that states that victims will be heard and helped. Two major components of an effective violence control program can occur as a result of these actions. First, abusive behaviors are no longer hidden but become actionable within the residential unit and the institution. Second, the perpetrator no longer can expect to be protected by anonymity or the myth of "it's no big deal" or "it's none of our business." Indeed, success is achieved when students help other students to resolve conflict reasonably and when, if an individual or group engages in abusive behavior, the perpetrators are forced to seek help and change or to leave the community.

A strong community base is essential, for there can never be enough security staff to enforce rules, as many crisis counselors as could be used, or adequate judicial settings to adjudicate all of the cases that can be generated. Violence in residence halls must be met with a vigorous intolerance and with permission to speak out about observed and experienced violence, not with the fear, paralysis, or subterfuge that immobilizes residents and staff and permits even greater violence.

Efforts to combat violence and its insidious effects cannot be concentrated in just one department or affected with just one program. Multifaceted, repeated efforts are required. But, if we wish to build strong communities, we must start at the grass roots, the residence hall floor or house, and, through residents, staff, and other institutional departments, we must create understanding, enable open discussion and reporting, implement policies through adjudicative actions, and strip away the concealing curtain of another "best-kept secret."

Summary

Violence in residence halls is neither unknown nor uncommon; rather, it appears to be far more pervasive than most administrators or students would care to admit. Residents are aware of the extent and variations of violent incidents and are themselves perpetrators of various types of violence that continued to go unreported. Programs for creating an awareness of the various forms of violence and its ramifications within the resident population and on individuals should be a major priority for administrators. Reporting of incidents must be seen by residents as essential to the welfare of the residence hall. Administrative policies for handling incidents must be formulated and utilized so residents can experience some resolution of the violence. Without these efforts, residence halls will continue simply to reflect the "outside world" instead of serving as developmental centers where residents can learn techniques for identifying and avoiding potential violence as well as coping mechanisms for managing violent situations if they occur.

References

Bogal-Allbritten, R. B., and Allbritten, W. L. "The Hidden Victims: Courtship Violence Among College Students." *Journal of College Student Personnel,* 1985, *26* (3), 201–204.

Cowley, W. H. "The History of Residential Student Housing." *School and Society,* 1934, *40,* 705–712, 758–764.

Durant, C. E., Marston, L. L., and Eisenhandler, S. *Findings from the 1985 National RA Harassment Survey: Frequency and Types of RA Harassment and Ways to Deal with the Problem.* Amherst: Division of Housing Services, University of Massachusetts, Amherst, 1986.

Kirkpatrick, D., and Kanin, E. J. "Male Sexual Aggression on a University Campus." *American Sociological Review,* 1957, *22* (1), 52–58.

Koss, M. P., Gidycz, C. A., and Wisniewski, N. "The Scope of Rape: Incidence and Prevalence of Sexual Aggression and Victimization in a National Sample of Higher Education Students." *Journal of Clinical and Consulting Psychology,* 1987, *55* (2), 162–170.

Makepeace, J. M. "Courtship Violence Among College Students." *Family Relations,* 1981, *30,* 97–101.

Puig, A. "Predomestic Strife: A Growing College Counseling Concern." *Journal of College Student Personnel,* 1984, *25* (3), 268–269.

Roark, M. L. "Preventing Violence on College Campuses." *Journal of Counseling and Development,* 1987, *65* (7), 367–371.

Schuh, J. C., and Shipton, W. C. "Abuses Encountered by Resident Assistants During an Academic Year." *Journal of College Student Personnel,* 1983, *25* (5), 428–432.

Stark, E. "The Psychological Aftermath." *Psychology Today,* 1985, *19* (2), 48.

University of Minnesota Housing Services. *Living in 1988–89.* Minneapolis: University of Minnesota, 1988.

Walker, L. E. *The Battered Woman Syndrome.* New York: Springer, 1984.

Wetzel, L., and Ross, M. A. "Psychological and Social Ramifications of Battering: Observations Leading to a Counseling Methodology for Victims of Domestic Violence." *The Personnel and Guidance Journal,* 1983, *61* (7), 423–428.

Ralph L. V. Rickgarn is principal residence hall director at the University of Minnesota and a consultant and lecturer on suicide prevention, intervention, and postvention.

This chapter explores the topic of sexual violence on campus, particularly rape between persons who know one another. Ways to prevent such abuse on the college campus are discussed.

Sexual Violence

Mary L. Roark

All violence hurts. Violent use of sex is particularly damaging as it strikes at the self-identity of individuals and at their ability to be in control of their own bodies and, hence, their lives. Violation through forced sexual activity is a humiliating invasion of privacy and can involve fear for one's life. Sexual violence is almost always accompanied by physical, emotional, and verbal abuse; thus, it has all the negative ramifications of the other types of violence discussed in this book.

As a term, sexual violence is not clearly defined either by law by common usage. Any sex act between persons can be considered violent when the act is performed by force against the will of one of the parties; this includes gaining acquiescence by psychological or physical threats. The most extreme sexually violent behaviors are the crimes of rape, legally defined as sexual assault, and attempted sexual assault. Other forms of sexual aggression include coercive touching and kissing, harassment of a sexual nature, exhibitionism, and obscene phone calls.

The terms *acquaintance rape* and *date rape* are used to describe sexual assault between persons who know one another. Gang rapes, where groups of offenders abuse a single victim, also may occur among persons who know one another. Most legal definitions of rape include three elements: (1) sexual intercourse that is (2) forced on another person (3) against his or her will. The relationship of the parties rarely enters into the legal definition; however, acquaintance rape is often not acknowl-

J. M. Sherrill and D. G. Siegel (eds.). *Responding to Violence on Campus.*
New Directions for Student Services, no. 47. San Francisco: Jossey-Bass, Fall 1989.

edged as "real" rape by many individuals and sometimes even by judicial processes.

Any assessment of the seriousness of a specific act of sexual violence depends on several factors: the extent of psychological trauma to the victim, both immediately after the act and for a period thereafter, the extent and type of force used, the nature and extent of physical injury, and the relationship between the two parties. Sexual assault carried out by a person one had trusted, in a setting one had assumed safe, may have more serious psychological ramifications than rape by a stranger.

The word *victim* is used in this chapter to indicate a person who has been subjected to an act of sexual violence. It is not meant to imply that the person remains in the victim state; indeed, many of the services of a college related to sexual violence are intended to remove the effects of victimization as quickly and as completely as possible.

Prevalence of Sexual Aggression on Campus

It is difficult to separate the extent of an increase in sexual violence in society from an increase in reporting such events. There seems to be clear evidence, however, of an increase in crime on campus in recent years. Firm statistics are difficult to attain because of differences across institutions, definitions, methods of gathering the data, and reporting sources. Most important, the lack of reporting by those who have been victimized has resulted in incomplete data. But student affairs professionals widely accept the viewpoint that any amount of sexual violence on college campuses is counterproductive to a healthy living and learning environment.

Recent surveys indicate the commonness of sexual aggression in the experience of college students. Although rape by strangers is most typically feared by women and most commonly responded to by authorities, it occurs far less frequently than does acquaintance rape and date rape. Rape by persons known to the victim accounts for 60 percent of all rapes in society at large, according to Seligman (1984), and probably is even higher on college campuses. Koss and Oros (1982) found that from 15 to 20 percent of college women have been victims of attempted rape. Rapaport and Burkhart (1984) surveyed college men, 15 percent of whom reported having had intercourse with a woman against her will; only 39 percent of the men denied coercive sexual involvement. Ehrhart and Sandler (1985) identified more than fifty incidents of gang rapes on college campuses in recent years.

The most comprehensive study to date on sexual aggression and victimization was completed by Mary P. Koss and colleagues, encompassing a national sample of thirty-two colleges and universities, with responses from 6,159 male and female students (Koss, Gidycz, and Wisniewski, 1987). Using the Sexual Experiences Survey, a self-report instrument designed to reflect various degrees of sexual aggression and victimization, the researchers found that 54 percent of college women claim to have been sexually victimized. One in four women surveyed had suffered an experience that met the legal definition of rape; of those raped, 84 percent knew the man involved and just 5 percent reported the incident to the police. Only 20 percent of those who met the legal definition of rape identified themselves as rape victims. In the same study, one in twelve men (8.5 percent) indicated they had committed acts that met the legal definition of rape; of this group, only one saw his behavior as rape. Twenty-five percent of the college men admitted sexually aggressive behavior.

Garrett-Gooding and Senter (1987) reported that almost 50 percent of the male students who participated in a study on sexual aggression indicated that they had engaged in sexual coercion, ranging from kissing a woman over her objections to using physical violence or a weapon to obtain intercourse.

Sexual violence on campus, as in society, is mostly perpetrated by males, with females the usual victims. Still to be ascertained is how frequently similar violence is experienced by college men.

Effects of Violent Sex Acts

The effects of sexual aggression are similar to the effects of other forms of personal violence. Cognitively, targets of assault lose a sense of control and have lessened self-esteem and a less secure sense of self-identity and safety. From a victim's point of view, rape is not about sex but about a confrontation with the possibility of death. Behaviorally, victimized persons often withdraw, temporarily or more permanently, from relationships and settings that were previously a healthy part of life; ordinary activities, such as studying and participating in campus events, may be halted or carried on in a desultory fashion; sexual performance may be impaired. Affectively, the powerful emotions of fear, anger, grief, and guilt affect behavior and interact with thinking patterns. A loss of trust in others, in the environment, and in one's own judgment often occurs.

Any of these effects may be experienced also by those close to the victim, such as roommates, friends, and family. If the rape was perpetrated by someone other than the victim's usual romantic partner, that partner also may experience negative effects from the sexual assault. The relationship itself may deteriorate, and future sexual closeness may suffer.

The costs of victimization and violence to an institution are high, and the institution itself can become a victim when sexual violence takes place within its boundaries. Of great seriousness in an academic institution is the disruption of the learning environment for an individual or for groups of students and staff; personal resources, capacities, and time are lost for those who are occupied with the aftereffects of violence. The institution also suffers the loss of positive image, often with an accompanying loss of students through withdrawal of current students and nonmatriculation of potential students. All of these negative effects carry a monetary cost, as well as a moral one, and there may be the further threat of legal action against the institution for negligence regarding personal safety.

Prevention Interventions

Sexual violence is both an institutional and a personal concern, with its prevention on campus a shared responsibility between the college and the individuals within it. There are certain actions that the institution, through its staff and resources, can and should initiate; other actions can be taken only by the individuals who are themselves at risk of being perpetrators or victims of sexual violence. Protecting individuals from harm protects the institution and vice versa.

Interventions to reduce or eliminate sexual violence must be taken on several fronts at the same time, as single solutions will not be sufficiently effective. Multifaceted, coordinated efforts are needed in response to the complexities of the problem. While preventive actions can be specific to a particular form of personal violence, there is a generic quality to prevention that is similar across the types of violence to which it is applied (Roark, 1987).

Institutional Responses. Institutional responses to campus violence are discussed here according to the level of prevention provided: (1) tertiary prevention to limit the damage of a situation that has already taken place; (2) secondary prevention to identify existing problems and to bring about effective correction at the earliest possible time; and (3) primary prevention to prevent new cases of victimization by addressing causes and changing actions and attitudes that contribute to the prevalence of sexual violence.

Although these categories of prevention are useful for discussion purposes, they are not so clearly divided in actuality. Individual needs that may seem to fall into one particular category may well be met by interventions in another category. Almost all prevention activities heighten awareness of the issue of sexual violence and, thus, may prevent further occurrences. Some activities, such as provision of information, serve all three kinds of prevention. Delivery mechanisms can be the same for both secondary and primary prevention activities; these same mechanisms also bring some people forward for tertiary services.

Prevention of sexual violence begins with awareness. Open and extensive discussion of the topic of violence on campus will, in itself, serve as a preventive measure by counteracting denial and ignorance. Such discussion can raise personal consciousness, help individuals watch out for themselves and for friends, and can limit personal vulnerability.

Tertiary Prevention. Tertiary prevention, taken after an incident has already occurred, attempts to control the extent of the damage to individuals. The basic concern is that appropriate services and support are given to fill identified individual needs. The network of assistance to move a person from victim to survivor includes, at minimum, the campus or other medical facility, campus security or city police, residence hall personnel, counseling center, and judicial office. All persons involved in incidents of sexual violence must be treated with respect, informed of options, and supported. Supports are also needed for those in the community who are affected by acts of violence. Specific tertiary prevention activities include:

1. Offer remediation of the effects of sexual violence through counseling and support groups. The needs of the victim must be understood, particularly the need to reestablish control. Counseling services are discussed in Chapter Five.

2. Establish reporting procedures that are readily available and that are sensitive and humane in operation. Survivors of sexual violence are revictimized by harsh, intrusive, disbelieving personnel to whom repeated reports must be made. Victims usually find it difficult to come forward; thus, there should be many places in the system where contact can be made. Victims, especially of crimes like date rape and sexual harassment in which legal definitions vary from societal norms, may need to be helped to understand the exploitation that has taken place.

3. Provide medical services to the victim, both immediately after an assault and continuing as necessary. Advocacy and support services may need to be provided in communities where medical personnel are not sensitive to the needs of a sexual assault victim.

4. Provide protective security services if necessary, to stop any repeat of the assault. Often the danger of repetition of sexual violence and retaliation for reporting are greater in situations where the assailant is an acquaintance and a member of the same social circle instead of a stranger.

5. Involve civil authorities, when appropriate, with accompanying support from campus personnel. Whether the investigation is to be carried out by campus security or local police and whether the adjudication is to be under campus regulations or under criminal charges are matters to be decided by individual circumstances.

6. Enforce campus judicial codes in such a way as to offer all parties due process while minimizing the continuing psychological pain of an assault. The college does owe fairness to all persons under its jurisdiction; one aspect of this fairness is the protection of confidentiality to the greatest extent possible.

7. Establish and/or cooperate with a rape crisis center or volunteer sexual assault service. The needs of the victim for support are great at every decision point; a trained volunteer can offer information, caring, and objectivity to supplement the support from staff and friends.

8. Create reporting mechanisms that fit local needs. Secrecy about incidents of violence on campus usually backfires. It leads to rumors and gossip sweeping the campus and making an already distressing situation worse. The timing and content of any public report must protect the privacy, anonymity, and confidentiality of both the victim and the alleged offender whenever possible. Annual reports can provide useful summary data for the campus community.

Secondary Prevention. Secondary prevention efforts recognize that a problem exists and that students form an at-risk group for sexual violence because of typical age-related characteristics. Secondary prevention seeks to keep violence from happening by removing precipitating factors and by establishing institutional policies to deal strongly with reported incidents of violence. Specific components of secondary prevention follow:

1. Inform students of security risks in the campus setting, the procedures they can take to minimize personal danger, and the measures established by the institution for their protection.

2. Establish a campuswide task force or committee for issues of personal safety, appointed by the highest campus authority possible and broadly representative of all campus groups. General goals for such a group might be to educate the campus community about the topic, to coordinate prevention activities, to identify and publicize campus and community resources, and to monitor the extent of sexual violence at the college.

3. Conduct research on local campus violence, with prevalence data gathered by a variety of means, such as official reports, self-reports, and perceptions of campus constituents.

4. Train resident assistants to set and interpret norms of acceptable behavior in student housing units, arrange for educational programming on their floors, facilitate the processing of complaints, and make appropriate referrals.

5. Develop and disseminate policies to prohibit all forms of sexual violence. Develop procedures to deal effectively, consistently, and firmly with charges of sexual violence. The language of present student codes may need to be updated to define ambiguities such as what constitutes rape in dating situations and to clarify that any form of sexual exploitation on campus is prohibited.

6. Encourage the reporting of acts of aggression, with appropriate safeguards to client confidentiality.

7. Create a campus resource center, important for its symbolic as well as actual value, to provide readily available information on topics of sexual violence and on the available services and support systems.

8. Identify problem areas in the environment and take actions to remedy them. Adequate lighting, secure locking mechanisms, emergency telephones, and similar physical considerations are valuable, as are student patrols and escort services. Most important is a trained security staff that is sensitive, fair, and considerate to the confused, upset, or angry persons making a charge of some form of assault.

9. Establish cooperative working relationships among staff members in offices most likely to be aware of the violence that is threatened or already occurring; these offices are most commonly the chief student affairs administrative office, residential life, public safety, counseling, judicial affairs, and student activities.

Primary Prevention. Primary prevention takes action before the onset of a problem; its major aim is to stop dangerous situations from happening. Education itself is a natural primary prevention tool to use in higher educational institutions "to promote better interpersonal, intergroup, intergender relationships on the campus" (Office of Educational Services, 1985, p. 14), which can thereby reduce the extent of threat. Educational programs add knowledge, which is a form of empowerment. They also reach many levels of concern: past victims, persons at risk, potential offenders, and caring community members.

Certain groups should be special targets for educational efforts because they are critical to the functioning of the campus—namely, residential life staff and peer counselors. Other groups should be special targets because they are potentially at greater risk—namely, women's groups and freshmen students. And some groups should be targets for education because their structure or nature or history have made abuse of power more visible, if not more prevalent—namely, athletes in contact sports and members of Greek social organizations.

Primary prevention mechanisms include:

1. Teach campus constituents about various forms of sexual and personal violence. Information could include definitions, prevalence, self-protection, campus regulations, sanctions, and resources for help.

2. Educate students about skills that will prevent one from becoming a victim. Among the kinds of skills that can be developed through workshop presentations are those that lead to greater control of self and, hence, of environment. For both potential targets and potential perpetrators of violence, the following skill-building emphases are valuable: assertiveness training, communication skills, human relations training, anger management, conflict resolution, self-esteem building, stress management, relationship enhancement, self-defense training, rape prevention, alcohol education, and counteracting abusive backgrounds.

3. Promote experiences to increase awareness and to address attitudes about the social conditions that allow sexual assault to continue. Like skill-building workshops, programs that encourage individuals to explore

their attitudes about factors that lead to violence have great potential for changing a campus climate and individual lives. Male students, in particular, can be helped to examine the myths and socialization patterns that allow abuse against women to continue. Relevant topics include: sex role socialization; understanding one's sexuality, desires, and limits; separation of sexuality and violence; appropriate use of personal power; and confronting discrimination.

4. Offer a varied and frequent array of events on the topic of sexual violence: speakers, films, forums, panels, discussions, pamphlets, handbooks, rap session, awareness days, news releases, feature articles, publication of local research, and seminars on violence in general or on topics related to one type of violence. To address the visual orientation of students, create local theater productions, psychodramas, or videotaped and/or televised "soap operas" dealing with issues of abuse. Displays, poster contests, bookmarks, calendars, mock trials, and TV commercials are other formats for prevention education.

5. Publish locally designed brochures on the topic of sexual violence in general or on specific form such as date rape or sexual harassment. While examples from other campuses are useful, the process of writing one's own material leads to greater definition of local norms and increased clarity about internal procedures and services. Content of the brochure could include a definition of the concern, advice on how to take care of oneself to prevent the violence, and information on where to go if one has been a recipient of such violence.

6. Continue the security measures established as part of secondary prevention to deal with existing problems. The same actions will help prevent new problems from arising.

7. Encourage teaching faculty to address aspects of sexual violence in their classes. Many disciplines contain elements where the study of the nature of violence is appropriate. Education about violence can also take place in specially designed single-issue courses or in comparative, interdisciplinary courses.

8. Promote a clear, consistent, firm antiviolence stance throughout the college. Colleges and universities can perform a valuable societal role when they create a climate in which a social stigma is attached to all acts of violence. Change can be created that will have ramifications far beyond the boundaries and time dimensions of the collegiate experience if the setting holds violence, exploitation, and abuse of power in disrepute.

9. Ask the president of the institution to issue a statement or statements that clearly establish the institution's stance on all forms of violence. Policy on this subject can and should be developed at the highest level of administration. If appropriate, the faculty governing body might publicly endorse such a policy.

Individual Responses. In addition to institutional commitments to eradicate violence, some prevention activities can and must be taken by individuals; however, it may well fall on the shoulders of the institution to teach these concepts to individuals within its community. Individuals can be encouraged to:

1. Take a stand against violence when it is portrayed or evidenced. The legitimization of violence that seems to be present in society is felt also on campuses. American culture includes many proviolent values and behaviors; our history, our movies, our fascination with guns, and, until recently, our hands-off stance toward domestic abuse give evidence of this point. Relationship violence has not been viewed as a crime; typically, the closer the relationship, the more violence is permitted to occur within that relationship.

2. Avoid combining violence and sex. Sexuality and violence are often entangled, with subsequent confusion and double messages. When sex and violence are mixed, the result is almost always the creation of a victim. The term *sexual violence* should perhaps be rephrased to "the violent use of sex," to make the distinction that sex is misused when other persons are exploited or abused by it. The combination of sex and violence does not lead to healthy outcomes.

3. Relax stereotypes about appropriate sex role behaviors, in one's own life and in one's expectations of others. Sex role socialization processes add to the existence of violence when males are socialized to be aggressive and females to be submissive. Ignoring the rights of others and denying one's own rights are equally dangerous, and these actions seem culturally linked with sex roles. The unequal distribution of power in traditional sex roles may encourage coercion and exploitation.

4. Resist hierarchical forms of dominance. The inappropriate use of personal, physical, or institutionally based power seems to be part of many commands and demands that lead to victimization. Sexual violence is typically more about power issues than it is about sex. Conceptualizations about the causation of rape have evolved from viewing rape as caused by lust, to seeing it as caused by aggression and hostility against women, to viewing it as a demonstration of dominance and power. Patterns of patriarchy, patronization, and oppression contribute to the acceptance of domination by those perceived to be more powerful over those with less power; some childraising patterns may also be a contributory factor to later violence.

5. Use alcohol wisely and be alert to the ramifications of its use and abuse by others. Many sexual abuses occur while persons are under the influence of alcohol or other substances, although no direct causal link has been established between alcohol use and violent behavior. Perpetrators often use the excuse of being drunk or stoned to reduce personal responsibility, to rationalize their behavior, and to present a socially acceptable excuse for engaging in otherwise prohibited behavior.

6. Be aware of prejudice and counteract it wherever it is found, whenever possible. Prejudice may be at the root of much sexual violence and victimization. Not perceiving others to be of equal value with oneself can lead to sexual and other violence. When discriminatory stereotypes are maintained and when personal prejudices form the basis for actions, victims are created of other persons. Rarely are equals exploited; abuse and aggression usually are directed to undervalued classes.

7. Report sexual offenses when they happen. Campus or police authorities cannot adequately address the crime of sexual assault when they do not have the facts about its happening. Stories without factual backup data cannot be used to bring perpetrators to justice. Stories told by someone other than the person who has received the act of violence can only be preliminary to having the victim herself or himself come forward. Until violence is reported, it cannot be addressed.

8. Learn to take care of one's own safety needs. While the responsibility for the problem of sexual assault does not belong to victims, the responsibility for the solution, at least on a personal level, lies partially under one's own control. To avoid rape by strangers, individuals would do well to avoid situations and places where they may be in jeopardy, such as walking alone through secluded alleys and woods late at night or being casual about locking doors. Persons have a right to do, to be, to dress, and to act as they choose, but some choices are wiser than others when it comes to protecting oneself from sexual violence.

A more difficult area than protecting oneself against an unknown would-be assailant is to protect oneself from assault by acquaintances. Clear communication is the best protection for this situation: to speak up for what one wants and doesn't want; to identify what behaviors one will accept and what one will not; to clarify what one means and what one doesn't mean; to speak up early clearly, and repeatedly, if necessary.

9. Understand the nature of the population. Particularly with the "traditional" or "typical" college student, we are dealing with a population vulnerable of becoming victims of violence. Such students are usually in a new setting that has a variety of environmental stressors. They may be distant from previous support systems and away from direct parental supervision. They are at an age when sexual impulses are making insistent demands; their age puts them in the group that has the highest proportion of both victims and perpetrators of sexual assault. College students are under heavy peer pressure. Their identities are not yet firm, their competence not yet established, and they often have mistaken beliefs about their invincibility. Individual values may be called into question by others among whom they live who are experimenting with new freedoms. Thus, college students are a population at risk for sexual victimization.

The pamphlet *"Friends" Raping Friends* (Hughes and Sandler, 1987) has further ideas for individuals concerned with protecting themselves from sexual aggression.

Conclusion

Because sexual violence is extremely harmful, primarily to individuals and secondarily to institutions, all possible efforts should be made to eliminate it from college campuses. Since sexual violence is both a personal and an institutional concern, both individual and administrative action are important.

This chapter has outlined institutional response via tertiary, secondary, and primary prevention interventions. Also presented were responses that individual students and staff can take. Although the prevention of violence is not an easy task, its component parts are already present in student development activities, and the mechanisms described to counteract sexual violence are widely available to educators. What remains to be done is to focus energies on the issue of sexual violence on campus and to create a climate in which exploitation is denigrated and disallowed. Such a climate is created by intention and by intervention, by concerns and by commitments.

The abiding concern for student welfare on the part of all who work in postsecondary settings necessitates the eradication of all forms of violence in the educational setting so that the learning process and individual growth can be enhanced rather than impeded. To allow violence to continue in an educational environment indicates a lack of justice, a lack of caring, and a lack of courage.

References

Ehrhart, J. K., and Sandler, B. R. *Campus Gang Rape: Party Games?* Washington, D.C.: Project on the Status of Women, Association of American Colleges, 1985.

Garrett-Gooding, J., and Senter, R., Jr. "Attitudes and Acts of Sexual Aggression on a University Campus." *Sociological Inquiry,* 1987, *57,* 348-371.

Hughes, J. O., and Sandler, B. R. *"Friends" Raping Friends: Could It Happen to You?* Washington, D.C.: Project on the Status of Women, Association of American Colleges, 1987.

Koss, M. P., Gidycz, C. A., and Wisniewski, N. "The Scope of Rape: Incidence and Prevalence of Sexual Aggression and Victimization in a National Sample of Higher Education Students." *Journal of Consulting and Clinical Psychology,* 1987, *55* (2), 162-170.

Koss, M. P., and Oros, C. J. "Sexual Experiences Survey: A Research Instrument Investigating Sexual Aggression and Victimization." *Journal of Consulting and Clinical Psychology,* 1982, *50,* 455-457.

Office of Educational Services. *Measures to Improve Personal Safety on Campus.* Albany: State University of New York, 1985.

Rapaport, K., and Burkhart, B. R. "Personality and Attitudinal Characteristics of Sexually Coercive College Males." *Journal of Abnormal Psychology,* 1984, *93,* 216-221.

Roark, M. L. "Preventing Violence on College Campuses." *Journal of Counseling and Development,* 1987, *65* (7), 367-371.

Seligman, L. "The Date Who Rapes." *Newsweek,* April 9, 1984, pp. 91-92.

Mary L. Roark is an associate professor of counseling in the Center for Human Resources at the State University of New York College at Plattsburgh. She chaired the American College Personnel Association Commission One Task Force on Victimization and Violence on Campus from 1985 to 1989.

Various approaches taken by those in college communities who deal directly with victims and perpetrators of campus violence are reviewed. The role of campus police or security as "first on the scene" is examined, and examples of "newly identified" victims are given.

Counseling Victims and Perpetrators of Campus Violence

Nancy Greene Cerio

Because the college is part of the larger society, it would follow that colleges are "societies" or "communities" within which one may see the same types of behaviors one sees in the larger American society. Violence can and does occur with alarming frequency at colleges and universities across the United States; what is not occurring with as much frequency is the reporting of violence on campus (Roark, 1987). It would seem that violence on the college campus, while indeed occurring, often remains hidden from public awareness and examination.

This chapter examines the counseling of victims and perpetrators of on-campus violence. More specifically, it addresses the following topics:

- Who are the victims of campus violence?
- Reactions of victims in violence
- What counseling approaches are currently being used with victims?
- Who are the perpetrators of violence on campus?
- What are the counseling needs of perpetrators?
- Police as first-line interventionists
- Special counseling considerations.

J. M. Sherrill and D. G. Siegel (eds.). *Responding to Violence on Campus.*
New Directions for Student Services, no. 47. San Francisco: Jossey-Bass, Fall 1989.

Victims

Who are the victims of violence on college campuses? On campus, violence can include such acts as rape, courtship violence, sexual aggression, assault, hazing, harassment, name calling, and so forth. Certainly, any member of the college community may be the direct victim of such forms of violence.

Three levels of victims can be identified: direct victims, hidden or indirect victims, and the institution itself. Women have been and continue to be direct victims of such violent acts as stranger rape, date rape, sexual harassment, and courtship violence. Certainly, men on campus are also subject to such violence, but women are more commonly the victims (Roark, 1987).

Recent changes in our society have resulted in similar, parallel changes on American campuses. Violent acts against minority and ethnic groups have increased over the past several years. Schuh, Shipton, and Edman (1986) reported that, from 1980 to 1983, racial conflicts increased. Reports of racial violence have appeared not only in the professional literature but also in the national media. As reported in the *Chronicle of Higher Education* (Collison, 1987), racial violence has occurred at many colleges and universities. The incidents range from racial slurs and taunting to beatings.

While women and black students as victims may be familiar and therefore not surprising to the reader, other less familiar groups have become targets for campus violence. While filming a videotape entitled "Fighting Drunk," a recent Dartmouth College graduate was badly beaten by members of a fraternity ("Michigan Meets Black Students' Demands," 1987). Ironically, the videotape examined the relationship of alcohol to sexual assault and other forms of violence. During a racial incident at Columbia University, two black security officers were allegedly hit by whites when the officers attempted to intervene ("Michigan Meets Black Students' Demands," 1987). An evangelical Christian faculty member reported harassment by fellow faculty ("Michigan Meets Black Students' Demands," 1987). Gay men and lesbian women on college campuses—both students and faculty—are victims of violence inspired by homophobia. As reported in "In Brief" (1987a), a Holocaust memorial at the University of Denver was vandalized four times within the week that the memorial was erected. As reported in "In Brief" (1987b), homosexuals encounter abuse such as death threats and harassing phone calls and letters. Incidents of fraternity hazing are increasing with over twenty deaths attributed to hazing in the past decade ("In Brief," 1987a). Age discrimination—ageism—is another form of violence occurring at universities and colleges ("In Brief," 1987c) often perpetrated against faculty. Thus, the list of "newly identified" victims includes: students who investigate and speak out against violence, security police, fundamentalist Christians, gays and lesbians, Jews, fraternity initiates, and senior-aged faculty.

In addition to "new" victims and "traditional" victims, handicapped persons may be victims of harassment and other forms of violence on college campuses. Students across campus may be direct victims of what Roark (1987) refers to as "academic harassment" in which faculty humiliate and intimidate their classes. Indirect or hidden victims are those people who have significant relationships with the direct victim of violence. On campus, that could include roommates, suitemates, colleagues, lovers, and so forth. Students often sue the university and college within which the violence took place, thus making the institution a direct victim as well. In short, violence, in its many forms, cuts across the populations of contemporary American colleges and universities, permeating social, psychological, and academic life.

Victimization—The Reaction of Victims to Violence

Much has been written about women's reactions to sexual aggression, particularly about college women victimized by acquaintance rape. In a study by Muehlenhard and Linton (1987) in which 380 introductory psychology students were surveyed, it was found that 77.6 percent of the women and 57.3 percent of the men in the study had been involved in sexual aggression, and 14.7 percent of the women and 7.1 percent of the men had been involved in rape. Since these forms of violence are so prevalent on campus, this chapter uses the sexual aggression model of the victim's reactions to violence.

Victimization is more than the perpetration of an act of violence on an individual. It is also a syndrome and a collection of reactions by the victims of violence. According to McCarthy (1986), three distinct levels of victimization exist. Level one involves the reaction to the violent incident itself, which has its own set of symptoms. A second level of victimization involves how the violent incident comes to be revealed and how the incident is dealt with by the victim and those to whom the incident has been revealed. The third level of victimization involves the individual's identification as a victim.

Because the literature suggests that the most common victim of sexual aggression on campus is likely to be a woman (Muehlenhard and Linton, 1987; Roark, 1987), the pronoun "she" will be used have to refer to the victim and "he" to refer to the perpetrator.

First Level. The initial level of victimization can be further divided into two stages: the immediate or acute stage and the long-term stage (Burgess and Holmstrom, 1974). Victims of violence are likely to experience a wide range of emotions during the initial hours following the incident. If the violence is perceived to be particularly intense, the victim may experience shock, disbelief, and numbness. In the study by Burgess and Holmstrom, victims of stranger rape displayed one of two types of emotional reactions in the immediate stage: the victims either expressed their feelings both verbally and nonverbally, or they were controlled, hiding their emotions in a calm manner. Often victims of violence will experience sleep disturbances during the immediate or acute stage. Victims may have difficulty falling or remaining asleep. Rape victims have been found to complain of decrease in appetite, stomach pains, nausea, loss of food appeal, and a combination of these. It seems that victims of violence, whether sexually, physically, or psychologically harmed, commonly react with feelings of fear followed by anger (Saldana, 1986). Those who have suffered sexual violence may also experience such feelings as embarrassment, shame, and guilt. Sweet (1985), in an article that summarized several major studies on date or acquaintance rape on campus, said that most date rape victims will blame themselves at first for the rape.

McEvoy and Brooking (1984) suggest that female victims of sexual assault typically experience confusion as well as guilt. They may be confused due to cultural beliefs that, after a certain amount of physical intimacy, "males have sexual rights over a woman regardless of her objections" (p. 31). The woman thus is supposed to recognize the point at which her male partner can no longer control his urges. Naturally, this suggests that the female is responsible for the male's aggressiveness and his inability to control himself.

Victims differ in the intensity and length of time they remain in the immediate stage. Generally, the symptoms of the immediate stage will overlap with those of the long-term stage.

Any act of violence is a disruption in the life-style of the victim. The disruption may continue past the immediate hours, days, and weeks following the incident and go into months and in some cases years. Burgess and Holmstrom (1974) refer to this as the long-term stage. A violent incident may disrupt the victim's normal day-to-day routine. Some victims, particularly those whose prior level of coping was impaired or those who suffered sexual or physical assault, may be able to resume only a minimal amount of functioning even when the immediate stage is over. They may remain at home (that is, in their apartment or residence hall room), may venture out only with friends, or may cease attending classes. Family may be contacted; they may or may not be told of the violence. Many victims will react by needing to escape or leave campus. Some may even drop out and move away. Those victims who have received harassing or threatening calls may change their telephone number.

During the long-term recovery stage, it is common for victims to note an increase in the number of nightmares. Content of the nightmares may include a replay of the incident or, as time goes on, a mastery of the incident. Victims of rape may also develop phobias, or irrational fears. According to Gilbert and Cunningham (1986), problems with sexual functioning occur frequently among survivors of rape.

Second Level. In the second level of victimization, the violent incident is revealed to and dealt with by others. Depending on the reactions and degree of support of those who learn of the incident, the direct victim may experience additional victimization. Saldana (1986) writes of the importance of the understanding of those in the "inner circle"—that is, family, lovers, and close friends. The traumatic effects of violence are "multiplied by neglect, lack of immediate remedial resources, and the failure of such support systems as the courts, the police, the legal profession. . . . Victims are not given the opportunity to recover from the criminal onslaught—they are repetitively dealt social and emotional blows" (Reiff, 1979, p. 75).

On campus, the reactions of various agencies can lead to the victim's revictimization. For example, in an attempt to be helpful, student affairs personnel may contact residence staffs, campus counselors or psychologists, clergy, health care providers, and faculty in order to "alert" them to a student in need. Such attempts to provide help and to pave the way for the victim may in fact strip the individual of a sense of privacy and may be experienced as a second intrusion. This institutional revictimization may be compounded by the now-informed "helpers" who repeatedly contact the victim with offers of help and support. Good intentions thus can become inadvertent, benign, and iatrogenic victimization.

Third Level. The third level of victimization involves the victim's perceiving herself as "victim." Up to this point, the term *victim* has referred to the individual on whom violence has been inflicted. At this level the person adopts the label of "victim" and lives out the role. The violent incident becomes the dominating and controlling event in the victim's life, controlling even self-esteem. In cases of acquaintance rape, the victim may now believe that she is a poor judge of character. She may experience self-doubt, anxiety, guilt, depression, and apprehension. She may begin to distrust those around her and thus lose her support system. She is prone to be revictimized in other circumstances and thus reaffirm her concept of self as "victim."

Counseling Approaches with Victims

As with victimization, three levels of counseling approaches fit with campus violence: crisis intervention, psychotherapy or counseling, and outreach.

It is beyond the limited scope of this chapter to review or introduce theories of crisis and crisis intervention. Victims of violence are typically concerned with the lack of control in the situation. The goals of crisis intervention are to assist the client/victim as she reestablishes psychological equilibrium and as she discovers new problem-solving processes or strategies, and to initiate appropriate referrals. Both direct and indirect victims may avail themselves of crisis intervention services.

In counseling, victims may focus on "guilt, anger, fear, confusion, stress, trust, grief, loss, self-esteem, and empowerment for managing one's own life without endangering others" (Roark, 1987, p. 369). Several types of counseling have been available to campus victims, including individual therapies, group therapies, and couples' therapy. The latter is most appropriate for incidents of sexual assault, acquaintance rape, and courtship violence.

According to Sales, Baum, and Shore (1984), the recovery process following sexual assault may be protracted, lasting several months and often longer. The authors suggest that younger victims are likely to demonstrate more acute symptoms initially while older victims demonstrate fewer acute symptoms. The older college victim may be likely to experience a longer-lasting reaction than that of the younger victim. Thus, crisis interventionists need to be sensitive to the differing crisis needs as well as referral needs of a range of ages. Sales, Baum, and Shore also found that, at approximately six months following the victimization, sexual assault victims experience a resurgence of symptoms. Again, the recovery from crisis may not follow a smooth path to a previctimization state.

Because the acute and the long-term emotional needs of victims require attention, a referral for follow-up counseling is likely to be in order. Referrals can be made as part of the crisis intervention. A relatively smooth referral may be enhanced by giving the victim the name of a counselor, by being present when the victim makes the initial contact, and by educating the victim about the recovery process. The referral can be further enhanced by inviting the victim to contact the crisis intervener following the first counseling appointment.

Burgess and Holmstrom (1974) proposed two models for counseling victims of rape that are useful for college counselors who work with violence victims. The social network model focuses on using the social network of the victim in order to strengthen her self-esteem and thus to assist her in the return to her normal style of daily living. A behavioral model of counseling focuses on helping the victim "unlearn" maladaptive behaviors, such as unwarranted fears and stresses, and helping her learn self-confidence by dealing assertively with daily tasks and expectations.

The cognitive behavioral counseling approach proposed by McCarthy (1986) is appropriate for all three levels of victimization. The focus is on both present and future thoughts, behaviors, and emotions. Past events and emotions need to be understood and dealt with so they do not negatively control the present and future. At the level of the initial reaction to the violent incident itself, it is important that the victim not blame herself or feel guilty. It is the perpetrator who meted out the violence and is, therefore, responsible for it. When the incident is revealed, the victim may need to explore, understand, and clarify the experiences of revealing and of others' reactions as well as of the violence itself. At the third level of victimization, the cognitive behavioral approach can help the individual to shift her identity from victim to survivor.

For sexual assault survivors, the involvement of the partner in counseling is important. Following a rape, counselors may help couples by: encouraging the partner to express reactions to and feelings about the rape; helping the partner understand the meaning of the rape to the survivor; educating the partner about the violence and the victimization syndrome; and offering individual counseling if needed (Gilbert and Cunningham, 1986).

Group counseling for survivors of campus violence may be a preferred option for college counselors. Survivors in a counseling group may be helped through the curative factors that are present in groups and not in individual therapy (Yalom, 1985). Through instillation of hope, universality, imparting of information, altruism, imitative behavior, group cohesiveness, and catharsis, survivors may: increase self-esteem; diminish self-defeating fear, guilt, and anger; overcome shame and self-doubts; develop new problem-solving strategies; and become assertively empowered. Although groups are often recommended for and by college counselors (Lewis and Cerio, 1987), the realities of limited resources, long waiting lists, fear of exposure, scheduling conflicts, academic calendars, and lack of training in group therapy combine to decrease the likelihood that this preferred mode of treatment will in fact be utilized on campus.

When an incident of violence has occurred on campus and becomes public, outreach becomes an effective counseling tool. Counselors can go beyond their office doors to reach those campus community members who might otherwise remain hidden victims of violence. Frequently, violent incidents such as rape, hazing, racial conflicts, and "ism" harassment harmfully affect more than the direct victim. Roommates, suitemates, floormates, classmates, colleagues, and other peers may be indirectly and emotionally damaged by the occurrence. Group meetings such as discussion groups, crisis groups, and support groups may be facilitated by a college counselor. This group outreach effort has been utilized by the counseling staff at Towson State University on several occasions following acts of violence. While no formal research has been conducted, reports from participants, hidden survivors, and counselors have been positive.

Perpetrators and Their Counseling Needs

While women do engage in violent behaviors, "violence seems to be a male prerogative" (Scher and Stevens, 1987, p. 351). Men have been socialized to be violent; and college men are subject to the same socialization processes as noncollege men. Men are socialized to internalize emotions, to be autonomous and self-reliant, to be competitive, and to withhold tears. All of this gives a clear statement to men and boys to eliminate or at least to minimize emotional expression. This may lead to violent behavior because a man may be frustrated when experiencing emotional pain with no legitimate, socially sanctioned outlet. Anger is the acceptable expression for men in Western society; therefore, violence may occur when emotional expression is limited or frustrated.

Shaw (1985) summarized research on university acquaintance rape, stating that sexually aggressive men are lacking in empathy, social conscience, and maturity. Women are seen as adversaries, and the men believe that it is acceptable to use force to obtain what they want. Date rapists have been found to experience guilt rarely, saying that they have not committed a wrongful act. College men who commit sexual violence may feel both frustrated and dominated by others. Men who are sexually aggressive tend to accept traditional sex roles, violence toward women, beliefs that men and women are sexual adversaries, and myths about rape (Muehlenhard and Linton, 1987). Date rapists repeat their violence (Shaw, 1985).

College men who engage in courtship violence tend to deny that battering is a problem, and they are resistant to change (Waldo, 1987). Both of these traits are characteristics of low ego strength. The batterer is likely to blame his partner. They are typically isolated socially and are therefore highly dependent on their partners. These characteristics suggest treatment modalities such as group counseling to help them learn to raise their self-esteem and to control anger. The group format helps these men break the isolation they have experienced and build self-esteem by helping one another. Anger control and assertive communication can be taught and practiced readily in a group. As time progresses, couples counseling may be an appropriate and effective treatment.

Scher and Stevens (1987) propose a five-step process for counseling violent men. In the first step, the violent male is encouraged to talk about his emotional pain and tell his story. A counseling group is suggested. In the second step, there is a relearning, resocializing of old patterns of masculinity. In the third step, the perpetrator learns the cost for the victim/survivor of his violence. Next, violent men learn of opportunities to feel self-worth, to be responsible, and to be in charge of their own lives without needing to harm others. Finally, Scher and Stevens suggest that the violent client must learn to forgive himself and others.

Police as Interventionists

Often, counselors, psychologists, and other mental health professionals are not the first college personnel to make contact with either the victims or the perpetrators of violence. Frequently the campus or community police are the first interventionists on the scene of a violent act. Not only do the officers respond directly to the violence as law enforcers, they also are frequently in the position of "helpers." How do the police respond? Anderson and Bauer (1987) have examined both the levels of law enforcement response and the effects on police of exposure to violence.

Police responses as outlined by Anderson and Bauer occur on one of three levels. Early in a confrontation there are likely to be low-level responses, such as an attempt at problem solving. The next level takes place when an officer takes direct control of the situation. The highest level of intervention involves the power techniques, such as the use of threatening.

Officers respond to exposure to violence, a stressful circumstance, by developing tight emotional control and an authoritative façade. They may become more suspicious, skeptical, and distrustful. A "macho" attitude develops. Perhaps because of this, alcohol use by police is alarmingly high and increases their health risks, marital difficulties, and potential for depression. On a long-term basis, police repeatedly exposed to incidents of violence may be at higher risk for cancer, heart disease, injury, illness, and suicide (Anderson and Bauer, 1987).

University police can attempt to maximize their roles as first-line "helpers" by becoming familiar with local and campus resources for the psychological needs of both victim and perpetrator. Halpern (1978) suggests that, with victims of rape, police conduct interviews with as few officers present as possible and in comfortable surroundings. Other suggestions for the police include establishing rapport verbally and nonverbally, using open-ended questions, being patient and gentle, and attending to the victim's physical and emotional comforts. The officer can be instrumental in recognizing counseling needs and in making such a referral tactfully and knowledgeably.

College counselors and psychologists can help the police, and thus indirectly help the victims of violence, by establishing credibility with the police. Once credibility is established, both police and victim/survivors will benefit from the counseling services offered by the university.

Special Counseling Considerations

Despite the prevalence of violence on college campuses, few counselors have received specialized training or are even familiar with the literature on campus violence. College counselors should become familiar with the types of violence that are occurring on campuses today, with the victimization syndrome, with perpetrator characteristics, with group therapy skills, and with consultation skills.

Counselors can be particularly alert to signs of depression and learned helplessness in women who are involved in courtship violence. Rape and date rape survivors frequently suffer some degree of sexual dysfunction. It is unlikely that a victim will raise this issue herself, so it is important the counselor be comfortable and ready to discuss sexual functioning. Perhaps the counselor will need to bring up the subject rather than wait for the survivor to do so.

In accepting referrals or information from others on campus or when asked to intervene with a survivor or perpetrator, counselors need to consider a central question. Just who is the client? It is the victim or the perpetrator? The referring individual? Or is the institution itself expecting to be the counselor's client?

In working with all parties to a violent episode, be aware of the judgments made, especially concerning the perpetrator. Countertransference is likely to develop in this situation, and, if left unexamined and not worked through, it could prove harmful to the client.

The developmental stage or tasks that the client is working on may interact with the violence in varied ways. Become knowledgeable of developmental theory and research in order to be alert to differing developmental needs of violence clients.

Finally, counselors can be especially effective in moving the client from victim to survivor. Using the term *survivor* rather than *victim* and facilitating client growth will increase the likelihood that the survivors of campus violence will develop or strengthen adaptive behaviors. In this way, counselors will have contributed to a decline in violence and victimization on campus and in American society.

Summary

United States colleges and universities are reporting violent acts with alarming frequency. Victims include not only the "traditional" groups, such as women and blacks, but also older faculty, gays and lesbians, religious minorities, and the handicapped. Victims of violence on campus experience a range of emotional reactions; in this chapter, three levels of victim response as well as three levels of counseling response have been described. Counseling can occur as crisis intervention, psychotherapy, and outreach. College and university counselors need to be aware of and responsive to the special issues that campus violence raises for direct and indirect victims, for helpers such as police, for perpetrators, and for the institution itself.

References

Anderson, W., and Bauer, B. "Law Enforcement Officers: The Consequences of Exposure to Violence." *Journal of Counseling and Development,* 1987 *65,* 381-384.

Burgess, A. W., and Holmstrom, L. L. *Rape: Victims of Crisis.* Bowie, Md.: Brady, 1974.

Collison, M. N.-K. "Racial Incidents Worry Campus Officials, Prompt U. of Massachusetts Study." *Chronicle of Higher Education,* March 18, 1987, pp. 1, 41-43.

Gilbert, E., and Cunningham, G. "Women's Postrape Sexual Functioning: Review and Implications for Counseling." *Journal of Counseling and Development,* 1986, *65,* 70-73.

Halpern, S. *Rape: Helping the Victim.* Oradell, N.J.: Medical Economics Company, 1978.

"In Brief." *Chronicle of Higher Education,* May 20, 1987a, p. 2.

"In Brief." *Chronicle of Higher Education,* June 24, 1987b, p. 2.

"In Brief." *Chronicle of Higher Education,* August 12, 1987c, p. 2.

Lewis, E. T., and Cerio, N. G. "Counseling Survivors of Incest on Campus." Towson State University, Baltimore, January 1987.

McCarthy, B. W. "A Cognitive-Behavioral Approach to Understanding and Treating Sexual Trauma." The Health and Education Council, Baltimore, July 1986.

McEvoy, A., and Brooking, J. *If She Is Raped: A Book for Husbands, Fathers, and Male Friends.* Holmes Beach, Fla.: Learning Publications, 1984.

"Michigan Meets Black Students' Demands; Columbia Rocked by Allegations of Racism." *Chronicle of Higher Education,* April 1, 1987, pp. 27, 30.

Muehlenhard, C. L., and Linton, M. A. "Date Rape and Sexual Aggression in Dating Situations: Incidence and Risk Factors." *Journal of Counseling Psychology,* 1987, *34,* 186-196.

Reiff, R. *The Invisible Victim.* New York: Basic Books, 1979.

Roark, M. L. "Preventing Violence on College Campuses." *Journal of Counseling and Development,* 1987, *65* (7), 367-371.

Saldana, T. *Beyond Survival.* New York: Bantam, 1986.

Sales, E., Baum, M., and Shore, B. "Victim Readjustment Following Assault." *Journal of Social Issues,* 1984, *40,* 117-136.

Scher, M., and Stevens, M. "Men and Violence." *Journal of Counseling and Development,* 1987, *65,* 351-355.

Schuh, J. H., Shipton, W. C., and Edman, N. "Counseling Problems Encountered by Resident Assistants: An Update." *Journal of College Student Personnel,* 1986, *27,* 26-33.

Shaw, J. "Date Rape: Dirty Little Social Secret." *Woman's Day,* May 5, 1985, pp. 88-89, 135-136.

Sweet, E. "Date Rape: The Story of an Epidemic and Those Who Deny It." *Ms.,* October 1985, pp. 56-59, 84-85.

Waldo, M. "Also Victims: Understanding and Treating Men Arrested for Spouse Abuse." *Journal of Counseling and Development,* 1987, *65,* 385-388.

Yalom, I. *The Theory and Practice of Group Psychotherapy.* (3rd ed.) New York: Basic Books, 1985.

Nancy Greene Cerio is a senior counselor at the Counseling Center, Towson State University.

A frequent by-product of campus violence is college or university liability. A case study is presented here, along with a discussion of liability considerations, the role of campus police, preventative security measures, and issues of confidentiality.

Pursuit of Knowledge or Pursuit of Suspects: Rights, Legalities, Liabilities

Christine Steiner

Historically, the college campus has been seen as a secure marketplace of ideas and a refuge from the real world. However, the realities are, and perhaps always have been, that a campus is as much a part of this world as any other community and thus is subject to its share of problems and tragedies. This does not suggest that our campuses are crime-ridden or that "campus violence" is prevalent, but such incidents do occur with some frequency, and they are sensational, highly publicized, and frightening. This may be because violence shatters the image of the ivory tower and because we somehow expect on campus a level of protection and safety that it would be unreasonable to expect beyond the campus walls. Because violence does occur, colleges must come to terms with the issues it raises: liability for the institution; preventative security measures designed to reduce or manage institutional liability; and the role of campus police or security officers.

Courts have generally rejected idealized notions of safety and have analyzed the realities of each case as presented. The ultimate question in any case is whether a violent incident was foreseeable and whether it was reasonable to expect protection from harm. Said in another, more legal-

J. M. Sherrill and D. G. Siegel (eds.). *Responding to Violence on Campus.*
New Directions for Student Services, no. 47. San Francisco: Jossey-Bass, Fall 1989.

istic manner, the question is whether the institution had a duty to the injured party, whether that duty was breached, and whether the breach was the proximate cause of the injury (Prosser, 1971). Included in this formula are factors such as whether the campus is urban or rural, whether it holds itself out as ensuring the safety of the students, whether there have been similar incidents in the past, whether the institution responded prudently to prior violent incidents, and, in general, whether expectations of safety would be considered reasonable. Moreover, the courts examine whether there is any reason to hold an institution to a greater standard of care than it would hold any other landlord when assessing liability or vicarious liability for the criminal actions of third parties. Violence affects all segments of the campus community, including student affairs administrators, campus security officers, physical plant personnel, and other administrators, and the obligations and responses of each division of the institution will vary.

Cases involving campus violence generally arise in the context of a civil suit by an injured victim (or by the estate of a deceased victim) against the institution where the incident occurred, alleging that the institution breached its duty to the injured party and that it should be held vicariously liable for failing to prevent the injury.

Campus Violence Litigation: A Case Study

The contours of the negligence standard have been explored by various courts in recent years. It comes as no surprise that campus tort litigation has increased dramatically during the period. Institutions have responded to this trend by reviewing current security practices and revising them where appropriate (Community Security Standards Committee, 1984). Few cases have been monitored with greater interest than the recent *Eiseman* case, decided by the Court of Appeals of New York in July 1987 (*Eiseman* v. *State of New York,* 1987). In *Eiseman,* New York State's highest court overturned a lower appeals court award to the estate of a rape and murder victim, finding that the state's alleged negligence involved no breach of duty owed to the decedent. In overturning the intermediate appeals court (*Eiseman* v. *State of New York,* 1985), the court provided guidance in resolving the conflicting interpretations in vicarious liability litigation.

The tragic facts merit brief review here. The assailant was Larry Campbell, an incarcerated felon with a history of psychiatric disorders and violent behavior. The court of appeals described Campbell's psychological profile as follows: "He was diagnosed as suffering from chronic schizophrenia, paranoid type, with a schizoid impulsive/explosive personality, a high criminal potential; he was said to have a potential for killing; and was characterized as antisocial, temperamental, belligerent, unpredictable, and disruptive, with a guarded prognosis" (*Eiseman* v.

State of New York, 1987, p. 610). Toward the end of his prison term, Campbell applied to the SEEK Program for disadvantaged students at the State University of New York College at Buffalo, a program authorized by New York law to provide higher education opportunities to residents who had the potential to succeed and who were "economically and educationally disadvantaged." He was admitted to the program on the basis of his written application. He began the program in the spring of 1976 and was carefully monitored by his parole agent. The semester passed without incident. In early June of that year, Campbell broke into the off-campus apartment of Rhona Eiseman, an acquaintance from the university. He brutally raped and murdered her, murdered another fellow student, and injured others with whom she shared the apartment. Her estate, through her bereaved parents, sued and prevailed at the trial court on the theory that the college was negligent in admitting Campbell because of his criminal background. On the university's appeal to the intermediate appeals court, Eiseman's estate prevailed once again.

The intermediate appeals court reasoned that the college was negligent in admitting and supervising one whose criminal past and history of mental disorders presented an unreasonable risk. The court held that Campbell should not have been admitted because of the obvious risk he presented and that his admission was the proximate cause of the off-campus tragedy. In its decision, the intermediate appeals court noted at the outset that the college could not be found liable for failing to provide adequate police protection because there was no special relationship giving rise to the liability; claims raising an obligation to provide additional police protection generally fail unless a plaintiff can prove a special relationship between the student and the institution (*Miller* v. *State of New York,* 1984). Similarly, the college could not be held negligent on the theory that it is in loco parentis to its students because the doctrine of in loco parentis has been long disfavored by the courts in higher education litigation. These rulings were not surprising, but the court concluded that the college was not "absolved of all responsibility for the safety of its students" (*Eiseman* v. *State of New York,* 1985, p. 963):

> Students enroll in a college in the expectation that, not only will they be afforded the means to derive an education in an atmosphere conducive to the stimulation of thought and learning, but also that they will be permitted to do so in an environment reasonably free from risk of harm. A college is not expected to be a guarantor or insurer of the safety of its students, but obviously is expected to provide, in addition to an intellectual climate, a physical environment harmonious with the purposes of an institution of higher learning. To that end it employs a security force and establishes rules and regulations, breach of which can lead to suspension or expulsion.

The court sought to limit its holding to the unique circumstances where a specialized program such as SEEK enrolls a high-risk population. This expectation of a reasonable degree of safety is consistent with the court's initial observation that a "college is not a complex of buildings nor its administrative officials but is comprised of those students which attend it, the administrative officials being there merely to facilitate the education of the students" (p. 962). The court reasoned that the college, having voluntarily undertaken the mission of educational outreach to disadvantaged students, has an obligation to perform with due care, including a duty to develop and enforce rational criteria for review and admission to the special program. "Obviously, if rational criteria had been established, a person with a history of violent psychotic episodes, drug abuse, and felonious assaults would not have been eligible" (p. 965). Clearly, the court expected that the program would heighten screening for admission to the disadvantaged program above that for admission to the regular programs. Persuasive to the court was the testimony of the admissions counselor that "[h]e did not know whether [Campbell] had completed [prior college] courses successfully, did not know his IQ, and obtained no psychological data, opining that such information was not required. He stated that he knew Campbell was in prison at the time of his admission, but did not know on what charges he was incarcerated and made no inquiry as to what they were" (p. 964). Pointedly, the court found the college negligent for placing an implied seal of approval on the student, allowing a convicted felon to join the community of students as one of them:

> Campbell's admission gave rise to an inference by fellow students that he was just another student who, as the trial court found, shared their "goal of experiencing the academic and social benefits of the college." It was, therefore, predictable that as part of the social interaction within the college, fellow students would befriend Campbell and invite him into their homes and apartments. It was also foreseeable that fellow students, viewing Campbell as their peer, would neglect to take precautions which might in other circumstances have prevented them from associating with someone of Campbell's background [pp. 965-966].

The court found the college negligent, even over its objections that the murder occurred off campus, that the victims had knowledge of Campbell's criminal past, and that there was no judicial precedent for assessing such far-sweeping liability.

Following the intermediate appeals court decision, the outcry from the educational community was swift and predictable. Colleges and universities were alarmed by what appeared to be a standard that was both unreasonable in theory and unworkable in practice. Amicus curiae ("friend of the court") briefs were filed by higher education institutions and associations.

In its amicus curiae brief, the American Council on Education argued persuasively that the brutal murder was tragic but that it could not have been foreseen by the college. The brief attributed three errors to the lower appellate court: (1) the imposition of a duty to vouch for the character and conduct of all students; (2) the application of too restrictive a standard of negligence, akin to strict liability; and (3) plain error in finding a nexus between the admission of the student to the program and the off-campus murder. The brief urged the highest state court to reject the unreasonably high standard of care and the obligation to screen where special populations such as former prisoners are considered for admission. The brief observed that the courts below utilized a thinly disguised in loco parentis standard—namely, that students were "inexperienced adults" entitled to rely on naive notions that their fellow students were harmless and fit companions. The brief also perceived the practical and obvious result of this strict standard for admissions liability: that colleges and universities would of necessity limit access to higher education opportunities only to those persons who posed no risk. Thus, the decision would have the unfortunate effect of foreclosing to ex-prisoners an opportunity for rehabilitation and advanced education. "There can be no doubt about one immediate consequence, adopting the special duty imposed by the courts below: no prudent college or university would admit an ex-prisoner as a student. Opportunities for higher education for this class of persons would effectively be foreclosed except in exceptional situations. Perhaps college communities would become slightly safer places. But released prisoners who would otherwise have attended college will still reside in other kinds of communities and they will possess fewer alternatives to a criminal career" (Brief Amicus Curiae of the American Council on Education, 1978, p. 16).

Not only is it unfair to bar the schoolhouse doors to ex-prisoners even after society has recognized that they have served their sentences and are rehabilitated but also, as the brief argues quite correctly, the standard, unworkable and unfair as to ex-prisoners, could only have the effect of being applied against all potential risk populations, including persons with communicable diseases, those with histories of psychological or discipline problems, drug abuse, or the like. It is impossible to imagine how colleges would screen or test for such potential risk without running afoul of constitutional considerations. Clearly, it would be unworkable and unacceptable to delve into an applicant's medical and psychological history on even the slightest cause, yet the intermediate appellate decision would have required that admissions officers do precisely that or risk exposing their institutions to significant vicarious liability claims. In fact, frightening for its implications was a statement of the trial court that "[s]imply put, Campbell posed as much danger to [Buffalo State's] students as a person suffering from a deadly communicable disease"

(p. 72a). This chapter discusses later the staggering confidentiality considerations presented by such a sweeping statement.

The court of appeals reversed the awards of the two lower courts, finding that the college was not negligent. The court of appeals explicitly recognized the argument of the educational community: "As the college and university *amici* cogently contend, imposing liability on the college for failing to screen out or detect potential danger signals in Campbell would hold the college to a higher duty than society's experts in making such predictions" (*Eiseman* v. *State of New York,* 1987, p. 616.) The court noted, perhaps with equal parts restraint and reflection, that "the question before us for resolution is simply whether the college had *legal duty* in the circumstances that requires it to respond in damages for Campbell's rape and murder of a fellow student; we do not consider whether a college might or even should investigate and supervise its students differently" (pp. 616–617).

The court did not analyze the question of institutional negligence on the basis of foreseeability of injury but rather examined, as a threshold matter, whether the college owed a duty to the plaintiff. The court rejected the claim that the college should not have admitted an ex-felon; it then rejected the claim that the college had a duty to restrict Campbell's activities or contact with other students. Finding no duty, the court could assess no liability. The court of appeals determined that the college's actions were reasonable in light of an applicant's civil rights to confidentiality and freedom of association. Even the lower courts, in assessing liability, had concluded that Campbell was properly supervised by his parole officer and that his release was required by law. Moreover, where Campbell had been satisfactorily monitored and the incident occurred off campus after the academic year had ended, the court declined to find that the college had a duty to its students. Thus, the standard articulated in *Eiseman,* following years of litigation and conflicting judicial interpretations, is that the institution must owe a duty to the victim-plaintiff in order for any liability for injury to be imposed. This will undoubtedly remain the accepted analysis in claims of liability or vicarious liability following incidents of campus violence.

Other cases involving violent incidents appear to bear this out. It is important to reemphasize that civil cases involving campus violence are relatively infrequent. Most cases are resolved based on their individual facts (such as those discussed at the outset of this chapter) that determine whether it is reasonable to hold an institution liable in negligence for criminal actions of third parties.

In *Miller* v. *State of New York* (1984), a nineteen-year-old female student was confronted in the early hours of the morning in the laundry room of her dormitory at the State University of New York at Stony Brook by a man wielding a knife, who raped her and escaped undetected;

she sued the university, claiming it failed to provide adequate police protection. The court rejected the claim, finding that the institution does not owe a duty to a student to provide protection absent a "special relationship" between the institution and the student, but the case was remanded to the trial court on the question of whether the college breached its ordinary duty as a landlord to take certain precautions where a risk is foreseeable or where there was prior notice of criminal activity. In contrast, in *Mullins* v. *Pine Manor College* (1983), the plaintiff was awakened about 4:30 A.M. in her dorm room by an unknown assailant who threatened her and led her through an inadequately secured gate, took her to another part of the campus, and raped her in an unlocked campus building. He escaped undetected. Evidence produced at trial showed that Pine Manor College is a small women's college of about 400 students. The dormitories are in a small compound enclosed on all sides by buildings, and access is gained through gates. The gates are locked from 5:00 P.M. until 7:00 A.M. and students gain admittance with keys. Visitors check in with a security guard at the main entrance and wait for the student to escort them. The campus itself is surrounded by a fence. The court found that a special relationship existed and emphasized liability on one of two alternative theories. The court found that the students and their parents had a reasonable expectation, fostered in part by the college itself, that reasonable care would be exercised to protect students from foreseeable harm. Second, even if the college would not have otherwise owed that duty, it had voluntarily undertaken to assume that duty and therefore must perform with due care. The duty arose not from an abstract student-college relationship but from the appearances of safety that the college projected—enclosed walls and locked gates, parietal hours, security check-in, and announcement of visitors.

The distinction, then, that can be drawn from these two cases is that where the plaintiff establishes the duty, as in *Mullins,* the court will look to whether the duty was breached. In *Miller,* no duty was established, and, hence, there could be no breach of duty and no liability. The final decision in *Eiseman,* in overturning the two courts below, has confirmed and clarified the principle of demonstrable duty toward others and should serve as the preferred analysis for courts in the future.

Preventive Counseling

An institution that is sensitive to the responsibility of reasonable security by presenting security seminars and by urging students to lock dorm rooms and use escort services will probably fare better in litigation than an institution that either puts on the appearance of a haven or that ignores prior crime incidents and the need for security precautions.

Institutional administrators can take steps to aid in reducing the risks of liability for inadequate security protections. The test in vicarious liability litigation is reasonableness and foreseeability. While prudent planning cannot prevent injury under all circumstances, a clear understanding of the institution's duty and the foreseeability of risk in light of that duty should minimize injuries and therefore limit liability. Administrators should be informed of potential and known dangers on campus. Appropriate warnings should be given, and corrective action should be taken. The institution should designate a specific person to receive information and issue warnings on dangers. Policies should be developed regarding immediate response to incidents, including medical attention, assistance from campus and outside police, and notification of family and others.

Recommendation One. Have a clearly defined security policy and a carefully selected, well-trained campus security force.

The institution should be aware of incidents that have occurred on campus in the past. Criminal activity should be recognized and warnings should be passed on to those likely to be affected. In some cases, extra security precautions may be required. Members of the campus security forces should be recruited and selected with special attention to experience and maturity, prior training, and knowledge of a student population. The selection criteria for security forces might include those factors that relate specifically to the campus's particular community as well as those mandated by federal and state hiring regulations. Professional training should be provided in first aid, weapons use, warnings and protection, crowd control, detaining persons, searches and seizures, and the like.

Recommendation Two. Have a security policy that includes inspections and maintenance on a regular basis.

Institutional officials responsible for the physical plant and operations must take reasonable security measures to reduce the risk of crime; these measures include providing adequate lighting, securing windows and doors, and minimizing naturally or artificially secluded areas. Routine inspections and maintenance should be done on a regular basis. Personnel who unnecessarily create dangerous conditions or permit them to exist after notice should be disciplined appropriately.

Recommendation Three. Have security seminars as a regular part of student affairs programs; they should be available for staff as well as students.

Self-protection and rape prevention programs should be offered periodically, either through the institution or local law enforcement agencies. Escort services should be implemented in high-risk areas on campus. In short, students and staff should be warned of increased crime activity and should also be aware that the institution cannot guarantee the safety of the college population. While this approach cannot prevent criminal violence on campus, it should provide the education and awareness to limit the number of incidents and limit the institution's exposure to negligence claims.

Recommendation Four. Balance adequate information to the campus community with the obligation to maintain confidentiality of records and communication.

An issue that arises with some frequency is whether, and to what extent, confidential student records can be released. As a general rule, disclosure of otherwise confidential information is appropriate only in certain limited circumstances. Although the trial court in *Eiseman* made short shrift of the confidentiality considerations, the concept of trust in confidential relationships is part of the very fabric of our society. Violating confidentiality may subject a practitioner and an institution to liability in tort, in contract, implied contract, or on the basis of a constitutional challenge, a statutory violation, or a number of other grounds. There is a presumption in favor of an individual's right to privacy except in situations of reasonable foreseeability of harm, and thus disclosure of confidential communications or records should be undertaken carefully and prudently.

The *Eiseman* court, like many other courts assessing an institution's liability following a violent episode, did not cite or discuss *Tarasoff* v. *Board of Regents* (1976), a controversial case that is not uniformly adopted. In *Tarasoff,* a treating therapist was informed of a specific threat to kill a specific victim who, although not named, was readily identifiable. The threat of harm was so clear to the psychotherapist that he informed the campus police of the threat but did not inform the victim or her parents. The court held the therapist and his university liable on the ground that serious danger of violence requires reasonable care to protect the intended victim. The court determined that liability is measured by the foreseeability of risk and the reasonableness of the action. The *Tarasoff* principle of "duty to warn" became immediately publicized and feared by mental health professionals and institutions that provide these services. The fear was largely unfounded, and the courts have consistently clarified that *Tarasoff* does not automatically extend third-party liability for the acts of others. For example, in *Thompson* v. *County of Alameda* (1978), the California court refused to extend liability where the perpetrator had made a generalized threat about killing but had not identified any specific victim. The *Thompson* court's explanation of *Tarasoff* should reassure any reasonable and prudent practitioner or administrator:

> Thus we made clear [in *Tarasoff*] that the therapist had no *general* duty to warn of each threat. Only if he "does in fact determine, or under applicable professional standards reasonably should have determined, that a patient poses a serious danger of violence to others [does he bear] a duty to exercise reasonable care to protect the *foreseeable victim*" of that danger . . . although the intended victim as a precondition to liability need not be specifically named, he must be "readily identifiable" [p. 734].

There are confidentiality requirements that must be observed with respect to student records, permitting disclosure only on a need-to-know basis. Under federal law, a student record is essentially any information maintained by the institution, contained in any form, that is directly related to an identifiable student. The Family Educational Rights and Privacy Act of 1974 (FERPA), known also as the Buckley Amendment, identifies two categories of educational records, "personally identifiable information" and "directory information." Directory information can be released generally. Directory information may include a student's name, address, telephone number, place and date of birth, major course of study, participation in sports and other official school activities, weight and height of an athletic team member, the student's date of attendance, degrees, and awards. Personally identifiable information, in contrast, cannot be released to third parties under any circumstances unless a specific exemption exists in the statute.

Certain records are not included in the statutory definition of student records. Of chief importance in criminal or potentially explosive situations are medical or psychological records and law enforcement records. These records are exempt if they are maintained separate and apart from a student's educational record and if other statutory preconditions are met. Records of a law enforcement unit of an educational institution are not considered student records when they are

- Maintained apart from the student's educational records;
- Maintained solely for law enforcement purposes; and
- Not disclosed to any individuals other than law enforcement officials of the same jurisdiction and provided that educational records maintained by the educational institution are not disclosed to the personnel of the law enforcement unit.

Equally significant, medical records relating to postsecondary students are not student records when they are

- Created or maintained by a physician, psychiatrist, psychologist, or other recognized professional or paraprofessional acting in his or her professional or paraprofessional capacity or assisting in that capacity;
- Created, maintained, or used only in connection with the provision of treatment to the student; and
- Not disclosed to anyone other than the individual providing the treatment and provided that the records can be personally reviewed by a physician or other appropriate professional of the student's choice.

Limitations on disclosure of records should not be confused with lack of action in situations of violence. Institutions should take swift action, consistent with their procedures, in instances of violence where the perpetrator is a member of the college community. These actions may include counseling at the first sign of a violent propensity, removing a proven violent student from threat of harm to self and others, and, if appropriate, initiating withdrawal proceedings consistent with the institution's policy and the constitutional requirements that action be taken in the least restrictive manner (Pavela, 1985). Each state, however, may have legislation that would pertain in these situations.

Conclusion

This chapter has made recommendations, based on court decisions, for how an institution might increase security standards and decrease potential for institutional liability. Also discussed have been the moral and legal obligations regarding records confidentiality and the court-coined imperative that reminds institutions of their "duty to warn."

Courts have struggled with the question of a campus's obligation to avert senseless tragedies and/or to take some responsibility for them. The highest court in the state of New York, a persuasive voice in the legal community, has clarified the institution's obligation as one of reasonableness. The institution does not owe a duty to a student that is higher than the duty owed by society at large. *Eiseman* (1987) should serve as a standard in higher education liability litigation in the future.

References

Brief Amicus Curiae of the American Council on Education, *Eiseman* v. *State of New York.* Gullard, Powell, and Steinbach, March 1978, p. 16.

Community Security Standards Committee, AICUM. *Report on Current Security Practices and Policies Among AICUM Institutions.* Boston: Association of Independent Colleges and Universities of Massachusetts, 1984.

Eiseman v. *State of New York,* 489 N.Y.S. 2d 957 (1985).

Eiseman v. *State of New York,* 511 N.E. 2d 1128 (1987).

Family Educational Rights and Privacy Act of 1974 As Amended, 20 U.S.C., Sec. 1232(g).

Miller v. *State of New York,* 467 N.E. 2d 493 (N.Y. 1984).

Mullins v. *Pine Manor College,* 449 N.E. 2d 331 (Mass. 1983).

Pavela, G. "The Dismissal of Students with Mental Disorders: Legal Issues, Policy Considerations, and Alternative Responses." Asheville, N.C.: College Administrator Publications, 1985.

Prosser, W. *The Law of Torts.* (4th ed.) St. Paul, Minn.: West, 1971.

Tarasoff v. *Board of Regents,* 551 P.2d 334 (Cal. 1976).

Thompson v. *County of Alameda,* 614 P.2d 728 (Cal. 1978).

Christine Steiner is assistant attorney general for the state of Maryland. She has served as counsel to Maryland colleges and universities and is currently principal counsel for the Maryland State Department of Education.

All violent behavior requires response from the community in which it occurs. Methods of response are examined, and factors to be considered are discussed.

Models of Response to Campus Violence

Jan M. Sherrill

Although we are college professionals, we are also interested in our students in other than clinical ways. They are our job, but they are also our neighbors; they elect presidents with us as well as flank us in grocery store checkout lines. It is important, therefore, that we participate in their socialization as citizens of a democratic community. Thus, when we look at student behavior, even those "scuffles" on the floor of a dormitory become increasingly significant. How acceptable is it to us as citizens that many students use violence as a means of conflict resolution? Awareness of the violence around us is an enormous first step toward preventing and eliminating campus violence.

Violent behavior presents special problems for a college campus, problems that come as much from how we perceive ourselves as from the behavior itself. The desire to believe in our campuses as idyllic communities of scholarly love and intellectual pursuit, for example, may create our ultimate vulnerability. An idealized community of scholars may never have existed as dreamed, but one understands the resistance of the educational community and the accompanying shock to its parent society to admit this self-deception and implied failure. To be aware of and to respond to campus violence need not, however, be seen as an

J. M. Sherrill and D. G. Siegel (eds.). *Responding to Violence on Campus.*
New Directions for Student Services, no. 47. San Francisco: Jossey-Bass, Fall 1989.

admission of failure. Instead, acknowledging the problem head-on may build our own campus communities and enhance the academic mission of the institutions.

There are many issues to be examined in developing appropriate responses to campus violence. This chapter discusses those considerations and presents ideas that may perhaps be implemented on all campuses.

Considerations in Responding to Violence

Size and Nature of Institution. It is clear that both large and small schools, commuter and residential campuses can experience violence (Student Services Office, 1987). But the nature of a campus's response can differ based on these demographics. In addition, the long-term response—the activity that takes place after the immediate response to violence—may be different based on the type of campus.

A large campus is made up of smaller groups—neighborhoods, so to speak, within a larger city or town. Acts of violence can have devastating effects on their particular areas of origin, but the resonance of violence, like disturbances in pools of water, may be observed throughout an entire campus. Therefore, a good and visible structure of communication is essential on a large campus. Student affairs staff and police may find themselves conscripted into the service of rumor control, of making certain that the truth of a situation is available right along with the rumor.

It is important on a large campus that violent incidents be made known to the whole community and not allowed to be "owned" by an isolated or seemingly isolated population. Violence does not belong only to the athletes who live in the dorms or only to certain races, and it is not limited by gender.

In short, whether a campus population tends to have only a slight bonding to the institution (as on commuter or very large campuses) or whether students tend to know and live with each other in a very homogeneous group (as on small, residential campuses), the college staff must direct the institution's response for the benefit of both the immediate and the expanded campus community.

"First-on-the-Scene" Personnel. On any given campus, any member of the community may be the first person to respond when an act of violence has been committed. When the victim of violence seeks help, the police, a faculty member or other staff, or someone from the residence staff may be there to respond. Often, these same community members might be summoned to or come across violence in progress.

The campus police will have a set of specific procedures under which they will operate; if they do not, they should develop guidelines that clearly indicate parameters of authority in dealing with violent incidents. Most campus police will provide special training, in addition to state and local police academy courses, for their officers. The best of these programs includes additional training based on the specific population they serve. Components may deal with date rape and courtship violence; racial awareness; fraternity and sorority awareness (such as knowledge of hazing violations); and violence against gays or lesbians. Particular emphasis on dealing with domestic violence might sensitize college police to the special circumstances of a campus.

Faculty also may be the first to encounter victims and perpetrators of violence. It is important that they, just as any other person not directly involved in an incident, be fully aware of how to report and get help for those who have been involved. An active antiviolence, public safety education program will include information for faculty, staff, and students who encounter violence. A good rule of thumb is to do nothing that will directly endanger oneself. Summoning proper authority is very often the most helpful action.

The residence staff is called on perhaps nearly as much as the police to deal directly with violence. Certainly they tend to know of more violence than is ever officially reported. According to Towson State University's Campus Violence Surveys (Student Services Office, 1986, 1987), more than any other administrative group on campus, residence staff found thc problem of violence to be one that their respective institutions could not handle. Short of treating some of these staff members for "battle fatigue," colleges need to be aware of the alienation and/or overinvolvement some of them feel. Residence staff may be the only group of administrators who themselves may be victims of violence. Even without being direct victims, a residence staff member may suffer from an atmosphere in which all levels of violence can and do occur. Utterback and Caldwell (1988) have identified posttraumatic stress disorder in student victims of violence, and staff can be similarly affected. Overreaction and nonreaction are symptoms that may be exhibited by an area coordinator or residence assistant. Again, flexible and clear guidelines for responding to violence will be helpful to all who may be the first college personnel to encounter it.

Student and Nonstudent as Victim and Perpetrator. Both students and nonstudents are perpetrators and victims of violence on college campuses. And, although the great majority of both sexual and physical assaults are perpetrated by students against students (Student Services Office, 1987), the kind of response that the college makes will be tempered by who the participants are. Nonstudents are often perceived as a threat, particularly by campus authorities (Smith, 1988). There are various ways of dealing with "outsiders," and the larger the campus, the greater may be the need for rules governing nonstudent guests. Some schools have made the individual host responsible for his or her guest's behavior.

Sometimes, as residence hall personnel can attest, the impetus for violence in a dorm may come from someone, at times a nonstudent, visiting a dorm room. Some institutions make clear to its residents that the same expectations of appropriate behavior are placed on guests as on residents; moreover, should the guest choose not to abide by the rules governing behavior, the resident host will be held accountable by the institution.

These institutions feel that it is very important to make the residents confederates in the responsibility for the dorm climate. Even though peer pressure may be great to ignore regulations, the host has a stake in guaranteeing the respectful, safe atmosphere of his or her "home." If the host is unable to control or tolerate the behavior of his or her guest, it must become the practice and the expectation for the host to ask the guest to leave; if the guest will not, the residence staff must be asked to help. This is especially true in relation to the use of alcohol when not in accordance with established institutional policy, and it is always true of using other controlled substances.

While such a policy may seem to be an expedient administrative solution, enforcing these rules can be quite difficult. For the sake of an institution's liability, however, it may be terribly important that all guests be required to register with staff before entering a dormitory. But uninvited guests to the campus may cause the greatest concern, especially for campus police (Smith, 1988), for it is this group over which there is the least amount of control. Also, for those campuses situated in areas surrounded by large residential communities, the temptations for juveniles to enter the campus for everything from student union video games to illegal drugs are indeed great. Large campuses may also be used as havens for juvenile runaways. None of these possible problems bodes well for an overburdened, understaffed campus police department. But, for any nonstudent who commits an act of violence while on campus, even if the act is not criminal, the perpetrator can be removed from campus and issued a denial of access or a no-trespass order.

For the nonstudent victim of violence on one's campus, the circumstances under which the assault or violent behavior occurred will greatly affect the college's response. Liability may be an issue, and, with that in mind, legal counsel will provide the best advice. Large campuses with a highly aggressive marketing or special events department most often deal with this kind of problem, and certainly stadia filled with emotional sports fans may present unique concerns for adequate management.

The larger percentage of campus violence occurs between students. This means that any college response must be geared to a homogeneous community, one beset with similar stress factors and one with identifiable patterns of behavior. We are likely to understand the milieu out of which this sort of domestic violence grows, and perhaps there is something to be learned from the way in which family violence is treated. Should campus violence, particularly residence hall violence, be approached as a practitioner would approach a family in crisis?

Whatever the case, the community must *perceive* a response by staff to the violence. Even in those studies dealing strictly with the likelihood of repeated domestic assault, when the assaultive perpetrator was actually arrested, fewer repeated their behavior (Smith, 1988). An intolerance for violence must be developed among those who practice it and who endure it.

Methods of Response

Campus Judicial Codes. Violence, perhaps more than any other type of student misbehavior, has an impact on the total campus community. Simply recognizing this fact is an important step. But behavior-specific codes of conduct or campus governing codes are not always a standard feature of campus life. The 1987 Towson State University Campus Violence Survey revealed that 5 percent of colleges did not have a provision for the emergency removal of a student from campus, regardless of that student's alleged behavior. Beyond the liability such nonaction may foolishly incur, the damaging message sent through the campus community may prove even more costly.

Behavior-specific codes of conduct have changed over the years to include prohibitions against assaultive, violent behaviors. Taking internal disciplinary action against a student is a viable, often necessary response. Moreover, courts have held that addressing student behavior with special regard to discipline is also the role of tax-supported higher education (Ardaiolo, 1983). In fact, some judges, in hearing cases of students charged with some form of criminal behavior, will not add to the penalties imposed by the college.

Helping students to accept responsibility for their own behavior is a built-in feature of campus judicial systems. Just as academic standards are set and enforced, so can behavioral standards be set. All codes are written, examined for legal sufficiency, and evolved from campus life. Provision for due process rights and channels of appeal can be, within legal parameters, developed or tailored to one's own campus. Each code will vary based on the needs of the campus jurisdictions involved. A set of provisions should govern whether cases are referred for criminal prosecution, handled internally, or both.

While some schools base code-of-conduct decisions on institutional history, on such factors as type of institution (public versus private), and on the community's expectations, we believe that each institution, particularly those with residents, should determine what is acceptable behavior for its campus through a consortium of police and security, student affairs staff, students, and faculty. Any violation of those set standards or expectations must then be met with an *internal* response. If the behavior is also criminal, police or security should remand the alleged perpetrator to the custody of civil authorities. But respect for the campus community and the civil interaction expected therein must be the first and foremost obligation of the campus authorities.

Too often such offenses as sexual assault, particularly date rape, have gone unaddressed because the civil authorities have a different burden of proof for prosecution than does an institution of higher education. This may be one reason why date rape, as well as antigay and antilesbian violence, is underreported. While we do not advocate the circumvention of a student's due process or seek to foment vigilantism, we urge each institution to respond in some manner to all reported misbehaviors.

Using Civil and Criminal Courts. Institutions that rely on the criminal courts alone to adjudicate and mete out punishment for violent behavior follow methods based on the nature of security enforcement on their campuses. Those colleges that employ a small, unsworn security force are typically very small campuses with highly restricted populations. This may mean that although violence does occur on these campuses, the administrative staff feels as though misbehaviors are contained or manageable. Many of these security forces operate as guards who, should something appear suspicious, have recourse to campus officials or local police. Often this kind of staffing is quite effective. On the other hand, an undertrained security staff may increase an institution's liability in campus violence cases.

Some schools use only local enforcement as the mobile security staff on campus. This literally means that the town or city police patrol the college campus as part of their "beat." This is most effective if used in conjunction with guards, but such additional staff is by no means standard. In such cases, the college community is essentially an extension of the outer community. The concerns discussed in the following paragraphs regarding the use of sworn agents as a campus security force apply, with one addition: local police have a larger constituency than just the campus population, and communication between local police and school administration may inadvertently be disregarded in any emergency.

When the security force on campus is made up of sworn agents with the power of arrest, a call to the campus police may be made from any constituent witnessing a crime or any constituent who wishes to report a crime. In addition, members of the campus community who can aid in an investigation of a crime will have access to the police. After reporting an incident, if it appears to be criminal in nature, the campus police can transport the victim to a magistrate and there swear out a warrant for the arrest of the accused.

We must be aware of two factors, however, when our campus police may arrest. First, students may be reluctant to call in officers or campus officials, for they may feel that arrest would be overly severe. This attitude may be particularly evident if the campus police are not fully integrated into the campus community. The second factor is simply the reflection of a national problem—namely, the often lengthy waits for adjudication within the U.S. court system. It is quite possible that a student accused of a violent crime may be released on bail pending his or her hearing and thus be able to return to campus. It is also possible that the district or state's attorney may choose not to prosecute a case. Unfortunately, this has been the situation with some instances of date rape and other sexual assaults. Not only does this present a possible continued threat to the victim but it is also damaging to the morale of the campus and decreases the likelihood of subsequent victims making reports.

When the doctrine of in loco parentis was abandoned, many campuses began to refer student behavior problems to local jurisdictions for adjudication. These problems could range in severity from simple theft to aggravated assault. One thing is certain, however: using the civil authority as the only response to acts of violence has helped to define criminal behavior within the campus community by bringing the outside community's expectations to bear on the campus.

Counseling. The specific methods and techniques of counseling victims and perpetrators of violence have been discussed in Chapter Five. It is important to note, however, that the act of recognizing violence on campus as a significant emotional trauma is, in and of itself, a valuable institutional response.

Without delving into interpretation of the law regarding emotional dysfunction, many college campuses have begun to deal directly with the *behavior* exhibited by a student and to respond to that as separate from underlying or root causes of the behavior. This has been especially true when dealing with students who attempt suicide on campus. While obviously the college is concerned with the mental health of the individual, it must also respect and protect the mental well-being of roommates, friends, and classmates of the student who has attempted to take his or her own life. Many schools now remove the student from the campus, pending an evaluation by the campus psychiatric staff or another qualified evaluator specified by the school. While to some this may seem insensitive, those schools who have such a procedure in place find it effective.

There are informal methods of counseling that also occur and are no less a response to violence. These methods are practiced most often in dormitories by resident assistants and other residence staff. What actually takes place is mediation between two parties in conflict. Some schools have formulated structured mediations. Trained interventionists and mediators are on staff and are available to meet with students who have disputes. The resolution found through mediation is binding, not unlike labor dispute arbitration. This kind of counseling will, of course, be most effectively used as prevention, with the intervention coming before violence has occurred; but, when the violent behavior is a first-time event—particularly in residence halls—binding mediation may be useful.

Disciplinary counseling is used often as a first response to some forms of violence, particularly vandalism. There is a formal aspect to this type of counseling in that, generally, a warning is issued against further misbehavior. Also, such a meeting between a student offender and staff member may be part of an ongoing judicial procedure. The content of the counseling meeting may then become part of a continuing disciplinary file and may be used to document the issuance of a warning about the student's behavior. As venal as it may sound, good record keeping with regard to disciplinary counseling can decrease the institution's liability should the case go further.

Deterrents to Campus Violence

Public Safety Education. Legal precedents show that public safety education affects a college's liability when violence occurs on a campus. Chapter Six is devoted largely to a discussion of just such issues. What colleges know, in essence, is that hiding problems of violence only increases their liability in all sorts of ways. Undertaking an aggressive public safety education program can make students safer as well as decrease liability should something unexpected occur.

One of the nightmarish conclusions many schools have had to come to is that no college is able to guarantee a student's absolute safety, just as that same student's parents cannot guarantee his or her safety in their home. What a school can do is decrease the risk of violence by teaching students to observe some basic common-sense rules. If administrators were able to get students to take the same rudimentary precautions that they take at home, the incidence of campus violence could be decreased.

Part of any public safety education is for the affected group to discuss problems or threats openly. This cannot be done without admitting that a problem exists and somehow seeking to understand or assess the scope of that problem. A very good idea is to make available to the campus community official statistics regarding violence. Where such record keeping does not exist, create that system. In addition to official statistics, conducting a survey to ascertain the campus's perception of the amount of violence that occurs is a good place to start. A model instrument is available for assessing those perceptions (see Appendix I). (Contact: Center for the Study and Prevention of Campus Violence, Towson State University, Towson, Maryland 21204.)

Naked statistics never tell the complete story, nor do they genuinely reflect something as complex as the total campus environment, but using campus crime data to foster public safety and decrease crime is not only smart, it is also honorable. Including basic statistics as part of an orientation program for both new and continuing students can be a powerful way to teach common-sense public safety. It also provides an opportunity for discussing the college's goal for the campus environment, which is directly affected by student attitudes and behavior.

Maintenance of Intracampus Records. Not only is it important for overall campus accuracy that good intracampus incident records be maintained but also, since no violence is ever truly isolated, many areas of campus life may feel both an immediate and a delayed impact. A dean of students needs to know about individual students' patterns of behavior. The student involved in a fistfight at the dance in the student union and the student who threatens an instructor over a grading conflict may be the same student. The dean's response to a series of incidents will often be quite different from his or her response to a single incident. The threatened faculty member, for example, may actually be told to take safety precautions if the dean has complete information. Public safety can be more easily promoted on campus when the campus is seen as a whole, with a central repository developed to house discipline files or behavioral information. Obviously, such record keeping is subject to privacy statutes and public information disclosure laws as they apply to educational institutions.

Relationship of Campus Violence to Alcohol and Other Drugs. Over half of the reported physical assaults occurring on campus involve the use of alcohol (Student Services Office, 1987). A much smaller percentage is thought to involve the use of other drugs, but this figure is far less reliable because use of other drugs may not be apparent to first-on-the-scene personnel. But alcohol seems clearly to be the drug of choice, and those students who do drink may have been drinking before they entered college (Upcraft and Eck, 1986).

Nationally, the figures may be higher; some say that up to 70 percent of all reported crime on a state-by-state basis is alcohol or drug related (Smith, 1988). Unfortunately, the relationship of campus violence to drugs other than alcohol is not documented. And, unless the information is gathered anecdotally, it largely does not exist. But the suspicion grows that the combination of alcohol with other drugs is increasing and plays a part in campus violence. Studies of just such a relationship are planned for 1990 by the Center for the Study and Prevention of Campus Violence at Towson.

Recognition of alcohol as a major factor in campus violence seems to demand an aggressive response (Goodale, 1986). Towson State University has developed a strong intervention procedure for addressing the alcohol factor in incidents of campus violence. A full-time alcohol counselor/educator has been placed on staff. Each time a university police report, residence department incident report, or university union incident report indicates that alcohol was involved, the student or students, should they be found guilty in the university hearing, are referred for a mandatory evaluation by the alcohol counselor. The alcohol counselor will then determine whether the student needs an alcohol treatment or education program. While both programs are available free of charge on campus, the counselor can also refer the student to treatment and education off campus, even within the student's home area for some who live far away. Verification of the student's attendance in one of these programs must be given to the judicial affairs office. That participation has become a component of the sanctions imposed by the assistant vice-president for student services. In some cases, when a student has been suspended from the university, the assistant vice-president may set the prescribed alcohol program as a condition for his or her return to school at the conclusion of the student's suspension.

At this point, the response has been gratifying. Students who have attended the campus programs through mandate have involved friends and referred other students whose attendance has not been mandated. Plans are under way to hire additional staff to meet the increased demand for alcohol treatment and education on campus. The university will monitor its own data to discern trends of alcohol involvement in campus violence.

The same procedure is in place to address use of other drugs by students. Those who are found guilty of possession or use of drugs on campus also participate in drug treatment and education programs as determined by the drug and alcohol counselor.

Staff Training. While some embattled residence directors may wish that they and their staff had been given combat training, the truth is that all staff should be informed about the amount of violence on a campus and some, depending on their likelihood of encountering violence, should be given particular training that addresses the issue. Understanding an institution's philosophy with regard to environment and violent behavior is an essential beginning for good training. In turn, that understanding is transmitted to students.

A comprehensive staff training program will include representatives from the judicial affairs office, police, student activities and residence offices, fraternity and sorority advisers, minority affairs, and faculty. Added to this list should be any office on which the impact of violence may be significant or whose direct service to students may be affected by campus violence. It may also be a good idea for a group representing all these offices to meet regularly to discuss current student behavior. Goals may be identified and plans of action created or modified as dictated by immediate problems and long-term concerns. Using both locally and nationally generated data (such as the FBI's *Uniform Crime Report*), this group may begin to direct its energies toward prevention as well as response.

Conclusion

Staff training is only a first step. In fact, sensitizing the entire campus to the issue is a major factor in preventing violence; however, building community may be the most powerful deterrent to campus crime and violence. A campus community will have diverse approaches to attaining its environmental goals. Intellectual debate and critical inquiry, essential to good education, can flourish only when the campus environment is conducive to discourse and respectful disagreement. Therefore, it needs to be said loudly, repeatedly, and consistently that no violence on a campus is acceptable. We must be committed to respond to violence at any level at which it occurs. Our perceptions, perhaps even our language, must change. Inherent in the description "just a little scuffle" is permission for and acceptance of the violence involved. Our concern must begin to be the generalized level of violence that afflicts the community as a whole. Many believe that for every room in a dormitory in which a woman is assaulted, there are seven or eight rooms on the same dormitory floor in which students are punching each other over whose turn it is to sweep (Sherrill and Siegel, 1987).

Students, faculty, and staff—all, in fact, who inhabit and enrich a campus—claim the fundamental right to conduct their studies and their occupations with reasonable safety. One constituency has no more right to it than another, and, while the degree of that expectation is open for legal interpretation, the expectation itself has never been questioned. The violence that threatens that expectation must begin to be seen as abuse, as deviation from the norm. Any community dictates the tone of its commerce by what it tolerates; thus, the campus community determines the quality of its interactions by what it tolerates.

Helping students to understand how much power they actually have over their own environment is fundamental to building community. Just as students know far more than administrators about how much violence exists on campus, they also have more to say and do about stopping it. The question becomes not "What can you, the administration, do to keep me safe?" but, more accurately, "What can we all do to keep each other safe?"

The problem must be taken up at all levels on campus; community "town meetings," student government, dormitory government, and faculty councils must all recognize and seek remediation of the problem. Success comes when students help other students to resolve conflict reasonably and when the individual or group that engages in abusive behavior is, by his or her own peers, forced to seek help and change or to leave the community. This is not nearly as utopian as it sounds. Indeed, what is our alternative? There can never be as many police or as many crisis counselors as could be demanded; we can never build enough courtrooms to adjudicate all the cases a self-victimizing society can generate. Violence on college campuses must be met with a vigorous intolerance—not with fear and certainly not with paralysis or subterfuge, as has been charged by some litigants. If we wish to create a better society, a better world community, we must begin by responding to campus violence.

References

Ardaiolo, F. P. "What Process Is Due?" In M. J. Barr (ed.), *Student Affairs and the Law*. New Directions for Student Services, no. 22. San Francisco: Jossey-Bass, 1983.

Goodale, T. G. "Conclusions and Additional Sources." In T. G. Goodale (ed.), *Alcohol and the College Student.* New Directions for Student Services, no. 35. San Francisco: Jossey-Bass, 1986.

Sherrill, J. M., and Siegel, D. G. "Violence in the Ivy." *Baltimore Evening Sun,* January 1987.

Smith, M. C. *Coping with Crime on Campus.* New York: American Council on Education and Macmillan, 1988.

Student Services Office. *Campus Violence Survey.* Towson, Md.: Towson State University, 1986.

Student Services Office. *Campus Violence Survey.* Towson, Md.: Towson State University, 1987.

Upcraft, M. L., and Eck, W. "TAAP: A Model Alcohol Education Program That Works." In T. G. Goodale (ed.), *Alcohol and the College Student.* New Directions for Student Services, no. 35. San Francisco: Jossey-Bass, 1986.

Utterback, J., and Caldwell, J. "Posttraumatic Stress Disorder in the Aftermath of Campus Violence: Strategies for College Administrators and Counselors." Paper presented at the Second National Conference on Campus Violence, Baltimore, January 13, 1988.

Jan M. Sherrill is assistant vice-president for student services at Towson State University and director of the Center for the Study and Prevention of Campus Violence.

A list of articles, papers, books, periodicals, and organizations that can begin to define for the practitioner the problem of campus violence is offered.

Conclusions and Additional Sources of Information

Jan M. Sherrill

Campus violence has added a new and troubling factor to student personnel administration. Few campuses do not experience some form of violence, yet few deal with the problem openly. Recent court decisions, however, clearly delineate the path of risk down which administrators may lead their institutions should they attempt to hide the problem.

There is no reason to believe that college campuses will not be wholly reflective of the society that hosts them. We may expect that our students, faculty, and staff represent a diverse cross section of contemporary life, and it is unreasonable for us to believe that human nature changes when people cross the "Maginot Line" of the campus boundary. Because violence can and does occur, we must work to prevent it and act decisively in response to it. Our goals must be to show no tolerance for it, to plan for it in our judicial and student behavior codes, and to involve our entire campus in security and prevention.

An additional concern of the editors and chapter authors in compiling this volume was that no easily available single source for discussion of campus violence, particularly none that attempted to encompass specific subjects under the generalized heading, existed. Other than a flurry of books and articles that have dealt specifically with student civil unrest of the late sixties and early seventies, the scope of literature on campus

J. M. Sherrill and D. G. Siegel (eds.). *Responding to Violence on Campus.*
New Directions for Student Services, no. 47. San Francisco: Jossey-Bass, Fall 1989.

violence has been less than imposing. The feminist movement has brought violence against women more prominently into recent literature, but there is by no means enough significant work being done on the cause, nature, scope, and prevention of all forms of campus violence.

What follows is a list of additional sources for inquiry, examination, and help. We do not pretend that this list is exhaustive, but it offers a place to start.

Harari, H., and others. "Group Versus Individual Bystander Response to a Violent Assault: A Field Experiment." Paper presented at the annual meeting of the Western Psychological Association, Los Angeles, April 5-8, 1984.

Eighty male college students were observed either individually or in small (three- to five-person) groups as they witnessed an apparent (simulated) rape. Such studies may help us to understand more about underreportage.

Lizotte, A. J. *Crime on Campus, 1978-1979: A Survey of 150 College Campuses and Cities.* Ann Arbor: Interuniversity Consortium for Political and Social Research and Michigan Department of Justice.

This is a machine-readable data file that includes statistics on violent crimes and property crimes occurring on campuses and in the cities and municipalities associated with them. Information is given on the number of police on campus and in the city, the total number of students attending the college, and the number of those residing on campus, with breakdowns by male and female for each category. The file is available from: Interuniversity Consortium for Political and Social Research, P.O. Box 1248, Ann Arbor, Michigan 48106.

Miller, B., and Marshall, J. C. "Coercive Sex on the University Campus." *Journal of College Student Personnel,* 1987, *28* (1).

This is a report of a survey of university students regarding their experiences with coercive sex or date rape.

Roark, M. L. "Presenting Violence on College Campuses." *Journal of Counseling and Development,* 1987, *65* (7), 367-371.

This article examines violence on campuses with respect to type, prevalence, and underlying factors. Victims are often further victimized by the institution.

Roark, M. L. *The Guide for Preventing Campus Violence.* Plattsburgh, N.Y.: Task Force on Victimization and Violence on Campus, American College Personnel Association, 1988.

This pamphlet was designed to help institutions examine their efforts to prevent campus violence. It can be used as an assessment device, a planning tool, and/or a reporting mechanism. It is targeted at interpersonal violence and assault, rape (including acquaintance rape), sexual harassment, and hazing; its generic approach to prevention can be extended to other forms of campus violence.

Roark, M. L., and Roark, E. W., Jr. "Administrative Responses to Campus Violence." Paper presented at the American College Personnel Association/National Association of Student Personnel Administrators Conference, Chicago, March 16, 1987.

This report looks at the types of violence on college campuses, the incidence of violence, and the effects of violence. Prevention strategies are discussed, and the draft of the American College Personnel Association's "Victimization and Violence Prevention Assessment and Planning Guide" is described.

Silvers, S. E. *Violent Crime, Hazing, and Arson on Campus.* Trenton: Office of Statistics and Information Resources, New Jersey State Department of Higher Education, 1986.

The extent of violent crimes reported at New Jersey colleges and universities during 1985, based on reports from institutions, is examined.

Zinner, E. S. (ed.). *Coping with Death on Campus.* New Directions for Student Services, no. 31. San Francisco: Jossey-Bass, 1985.

A college campus itself is a secondary victim of violence done to a student. This book handles quite well aspects of grieving and bereavement, issues that are also raised by violence.

Organizations

American College Personnel Association's Commission One Task Force on Victimization and Violence on Campus
Center for Human Resources
State University of New York, Plattsburgh
Plattsburgh, New York 12901
Dr. Mary L. Roark, Chair

Center for the Study and Prevention of Campus Violence
Student Services Division
Towson State University
Towson, Maryland 21204
Dorothy G. Siegel, Jan M. Sherrill, Robert B. Cave II

Committee to Halt Useless College Killings (C.H.U.C.K.)
P.O. Box 188
Sayville, New York 11782
Eileen Stevens
(C.H.U.C.K. is a prime resource for information about violent fraternity and sorority hazing.)

National Gay and Lesbian Task Force
1517 U Street, N.W.
Washington, D.C. 20009
Kevin Berrill, Director

The National Institute Against Prejudice and Violence
525 West Redwood Street
Baltimore, Maryland 21201
Joan Weiss, Director

Project on the Status and Education of Women
Association of American Colleges
1818 R Street, N.W.
Washington, D.C. 20009

The Southside Community Project
University of California at Berkeley
2470 Telegraph Avenue, 2nd Floor
Berkeley, California 94704
(This organization was formed by the university and the surrounding community to address issues of common concern.)

Sunny Von Bulow National Victim Advocacy Center
307 West 7th Street, Suite 1001
Fort Worth, Texas 76102
Cindy Arbelbide, Director

Videotapes

The following list of videotapes may be helpful in promoting or planning prevention programs.

1. "Acquaintance Rape"—Produced by students at Pennsylvania's Swarthmore College, this video contains two vignettes: "The Party" and "The Dorm." Each depicts the emotional and psychological aspects of sexual coercion.

2. "From Victim to Survivor"—This video explores how sexual assaults occur, the devastating impact of these experiences, and the slow climb back to self-worth and recovery that has made each victim a

survivor. It is available from Boulder County Rape Crisis Team, Boulder, Colorado.

3. "Not A Sanctuary"—This videotape deals with campus security and offers concrete suggestions to the viewer for effective assault prevention. The program investigates four incidents covering voyeurism, exhibitionism, date rape, and an attempted abduction at gunpoint. It is available from Instructional Media Resources, University of Maryland Baltimore County, Catonsville, Maryland.

4. "Rethinking Rape"—This program takes an in-depth look at acquaintance rape and its social causes. It examines our cultural attitudes toward women, female-male relationships, and rape. It is available from Contact Film Distribution Center, Seattle, Washington.

5. "Sexual Harassment: A Discussion Tape"—This tape provides an overview of policy developed at the State University of New York College at Plattsburgh and portrays five situations that may or may not be sexually harassing. It concludes with actions that can be taken if one believes he or she is a victim of sexual harassment.

6. "Someone You Know: Acquaintance Rape"—This sensitive documentary, produced and hosted by Collin Siedor, looks at the single most underreported crime in America, examines its effects on victims, probes the underlying causes behind the violent acts, and explores what can be done to prevent the crime and aid the victims. It is available from Coronet/MTI Film and Video, Deerfield, Illinois.

7. "The Beast Within"—Set on a college campus, this video depicts a counseling session in which a student is forced to confront those characteristics in himself that make it impossible for him to avoid violent reactions and that have caused him to put his wife in the hospital. It is available from Dapsho Video Productions, Pullman, Washington.

8. "Valentines and Violence"—This tape, produced by the Committee on Student Relationship Violence at State University of New York College at Brockport, addresses student relationship violence in a "Donahue-like" format with a panel of experts on areas of violence.

9. "You Are the Game: Sexual Harassment on Campus"—This video dramatizes the situations of two women college students who have experienced different forms of harassment. Most of the discussion focuses on the difficulty students have when dealing in isolation with a pattern of harassment, and the impact such harassment has on their lives. It is available from the Office of Women's Affairs, Indiana University, Bloomington, Indiana.

Conference Reports

The following are a few of the papers presented at the First National Conference on Campus Violence, Baltimore, January 6–8, 1987. For a more complete listing, contact the Center for the Study and Prevention of Campus Violence, Towson State University, Towson, Maryland 21204.

Rickgarn, R.L.V. "Violence and Suicide: Deadly Connections." Paper presented at the First National Conference on Campus Violence, Baltimore, January 7, 1987.

This paper focuses on the relationship between violence and suicide, demonstrating that violence has a far more pervasive impact on an individual's life and often begets violence by the individual against himself or herself.

Roark, M. L., and Eldridge, W. "Students Who Cry 'Wolf': Dealing with Students Who Falsely Claim to be Victims of Violence." Paper presented at the First National Conference on Campus Violence, Baltimore, January 7, 1987.

One of the unfortunate by-products of the increased awareness and attention given to violence on campus has been the apparent rise in the numbers of students who falsely claim to have been victimized. This paper gives consideration to the dynamics of such a situation and describes investigative techniques, parental consultation, and counseling interventions. Guidelines for faculty and staff to protect themselves from false accusations are given.

Walsh, C. P. "Date Acquaintance Rape Education (D.A.R.E.)." Paper presented at the First National Conference on Campus Violence, Baltimore, January 7, 1987.

This paper examines the cultural causes of date or acquaintance rape and the dynamics involved. It describes a model program that uses various methods to educate a campus community.

The following are a few of the papers presented at the Second National Conference on Campus Violence, Baltimore, January 12-14, 1988. For a more complete listing, contact the Center for the Study and Prevention of Campus Violence, Towson State University, Towson, Maryland 21204.

Asbury, J. "Increasing Understanding Between Sexes: A Workshop for the Greek Community." Paper presented at the Second National Conference on Campus Violence, Baltimore, January 12, 1988.

For three years, workshops have been run in a target area—the Greek community—about sexual harassment and sexual communication. Critical to the success of these educational programs was the use of credible role models for the Greek students. Role models included coaches, alumni, and students. These students and staff underwent an intensive period of training and a careful selection process to be prepared for running these workshops. Student evaluations of the workshops have been exceptional, and the program is now being expanded to other target areas.

Betlem, M., and Palmer, P. "Relationship Violence Training for Residence Hall Staff." Paper presented at the Second National Conference on Campus Violence, Baltimore, January 12, 1988.

This paper describes a program that acquaints residence hall staff with the dynamics of abusive relationships. The authors discuss profiles, warning signs, and various types of abuse. The program also gives basic guidelines on how to intervene with couples and help abusers deal with their anger.

DiLapi, E. M., and Wells, R. S. "Responding to Rape: The Penn Experience." Paper presented at the Second National Conference on Campus Violence, Baltimore, January 13, 1988.

This paper provides an overview of prevention and crisis intervention services developed at the University of Pennsylvania over the past fifteen years. Specifically, the role of the Penn Women's Center and the Victim Support and Prevention Services Office in responding to rape are explored. The Campus and Community Network of rape survivor support resources is outlined, and a three-part educational program for addressing acquaintance rape on campus is presented.

Dyer, C. S. "Working with the News Media on Sexual Assault Issues." Paper presented at the Second National Conference on Campus Violence, Baltimore, January 12, 1988.

This paper addresses relationships with the news media with regard to sexual assault prevention programs and news about incidents of sexual assault. The program considers how campus staff can develop and maintain relationships with the media to educate media staff, provide information, and respond to media inquiries. Examples of prevention program materials are presented.

Follansbee, P., and Betlem, M. "Exploring the Role of Alcohol in Relationship Violence." Paper presented at the Second National Conference on Campus Violence, Baltimore, January 12, 1988.

This paper explores what both the literature and experience as college personnel have taught the authors about the relationships between alcohol consumption and the incidence of courtship violence and acquaintance rape on campus. Examples from specific cases illustrating alcohol and violence, as well as profiles of violent and drinking behavior, are included.

Gray, M. O., Lesser, D., Rebach, H., and Bounds, C. "Sexual Aggression and Victimization: A Local Perspective." Paper presented at the Second National Conference on Campus Violence, Baltimore, January 12, 1988.

The extent of sexual aggression and victimization (rape, attempted rape, forced sexual contact, and sexual manipulation) at three colleges on the eastern shore of Maryland was determined with the use of the Sexual Experience Survey. Four hundred thirty students participated in the study. Additional information about the rape was obtained from female victims. Results support previous findings of high rates of female sexual victimization and male sexual aggression. Vulnerability factors and rape victim disclosure are presented. Implications from the health, education, counseling, and criminal justice perspectives are discussed.

True, J. A. "Campus Violence Prevented by Setting Security Standards." Paper presented at the Second National Conference on Campus Violence, Baltimore, January 13, 1988.

Preventing campus violence means the institution must: establish and set a reasonable, recognized level of security; assign administrative responsibility; establish campus access rules and guidelines; instruct all members of the college community in the need for standards; train security personnel; monitor performance; and keep the member of the campus community advised about security needs and activities and thereby avert violence on the college campus. Security guidelines include that range of activity on campus extending from residence hall monitors, through students and academic personnel, to campus public safety officers, and on to municipal police authority as needed.

Utterback, J., and Caldwell, J. "Posttraumatic Stress Disorder in the Aftermath of Campus Violence: Strategies for College Administrators and Counselors." Paper presented at the Second National Conference on Campus Violence, Baltimore, January 13, 1988.

The realities of date rape, racial conflicts, assaults, and similar acts of violence are often more profound than described to school officials. As noted in Vietnam veterans, posttraumatic stress disorder (PTSD) is a delayed reaction that may also develop in spouses and close relations of victims who did not experience the trauma itself. Clinical manifestations of PTSD, successful treatment modalities, and referral sources are discussed. A plan to meet the needs of PTSD victims systematically is presented with specific emphasis on the prevention of "secondary injury" caused by inappropriate reactions from police, administrators, and counselors. Proposals include interfacing counseling personnel with the disciplinary process.

Jan M. Sherrill is assistant vice-president for student services at Towson State University and director of the Center for the Study and Prevention of Campus Violence.

Appendix I
Intrauniversity Violence Survey

Fall 1987

Demographics (please check the appropriate items):

____ Resident student	____ Faculty ____ Staff
____ Commuter student	____ Part-time ____ Full-time
____ Freshman ____ Junior	____ Contractual
____ Sophomore ____ Senior	Number of years working at TSU
____ Graduate Student	____ 0–5 ____ 6–10 ____ 11–20 ____ 21+
____ Full-time ____ Part-time	
____ Transfer student (first-year)	

---

1. Are you aware of sexual assaults or rapes having occurred on this campus? ____ Yes ____ No
   If yes, how many? ____ 1-5 ____ 6-10 ____ 11-15 ____ 16+
2. Are you aware of physical assaults/fistfights, use of knives, or use of other weapons having occurred on this campus? ____ Yes ____ No
   If yes, how many? ____ 1-5 ____ 6-10 ____ 11-15 ____ 16+
3. Are you aware of acts of vandalism having occurred on this campus? ____ Yes ____ No
   If yes, how many? ____ 1-5 ____ 6-10 ____ 11-15 ____ 16+

4a. Generally, do you feel safe on campus? ____ Yes ____ No
 b. Are there specific areas or buildings where you feel unsafe? ____ Yes ____ No
   If yes, please specify. ________________________________

5a. Have you ever felt frightened, threatened, or intimidated by the behavior of someone on this campus? ____ Yes ____ No
 b. Was the person who frightened, threatened, or intimidated you: ____ A student ____ Faculty ____ Staff

6a. Have you ever reported a criminal incident to the university officials/police? ____ Yes ____ No
 b. If you reported it to the police, did it result in criminal charges being placed against the assailant? ____ Yes ____ No
 c. If you reported it to university officials, was judicial action taken against the assailant? ____ Yes ____ No
 d. If you failed to report an incident, check off the reason.
   ____ Embarrassment/humiliation ____ Fear of retaliation
   ____ No real damage ____ Nothing would be done ____ Other

7a. Have you personally been the victim of a sexual assault? ____ Yes ____ No

b. At the time of your victimization, had you been drinking or using other drugs? ____ Yes ____ No

c. Were you in the company of your assailant prior to the assault? ____ Yes ____ No

d. Did you know your assailant? ____ Yes ____ No

e. Was the assailant(s): ____ A friend ____ A stranger ____ Someone you had seen before

f. To your knowledge, was the assailant(s): ____ Student ____ Faculty ____ Staff

g. Where did the assault take place?
____ Residence halls ____ Academic building ____ University union
____ Campus grounds ____ Other campus buildings ____ Off campus

h. When did the assault occur? ____ Fall ____ Spring ____ Summer

i. Day of the week:
____ Mon ____ Tues ____ Wed ____ Thurs ____ Fri ____ Sat ____ Sun

j. Time: ____ Night ____ Day

k. Was your assailant: ____ White ____ Black ____ Other
Was your assailant: ____ Male ____ Female

l. To your knowledge, had the assailant been drinking or using other drugs? ____ Yes ____ No

8a. Have you personally been the victim of a physical assault? ____ Yes ____ No ____ More than once

b. At the time of your victimization, had you been drinking or using other drugs? ____ Yes ____ No

c. Were you in the company of your assailant prior to the assault? ____ Yes ____ No

d. Did you know your assailant? ____ Yes ____ No

e. Was the assailant(s): ____ A friend ____ A stranger ____ Someone you had seen before

f. To your knowledge, was the assailant(s) ____ Student ____ Faculty ____ Staff

g. Where did the assault take place?
____ Residence halls ____ Academic building ____ University union
____ Campus grounds ____ Other campus buildings ____ Off-campus

h. When did the assault occur? ____ Fall ____ Spring ____ Summer

i. Day of the week:
____ Mon ____ Tues ____ Wed ____ Thurs ____ Fri ____ Sat ____ Sun

j. Time: ____ Night ____ Day

k. Was your assailant: ____ White ____ Black ____ Other
Was your assailant: ____ Male ____ Female

l. To your knowledge, had the assailant been drinking or using other drugs? ____ Yes ____ No

9a. Are you aware of students who have weapons in their possession on campus? ____ Yes ____ No

b. If yes, what weapons do they have? ____ Gun ____ Knife ____ Other

c. Are you aware of faculty or staff who have weapons in their possession on campus? ____ Yes ____ No

d. If yes, what weapons do they have? ____ Gun ____ Knife ____ Other

10. Have you ever been threatened on campus? ____ Yes ____ No

Appendix II
Campus Violence Survey

1987 National Demographic Information

A. Size of institution
   1. Less than 1,000 students
   2. 1,000 to 4,999 students
   3. 5,000 to 9,999 students
   4. 10,000 to 14,999 students
   5. 15,000 to 19,999 students
   6. 20,000 or more students — A ______

B. In what geographic region is your institution located?
   1. Northeast
   2. Middle Atlantic
   3. Southeast
   4. Midwest
   5. Northwest
   6. West Coast
   7. Southwest — B ______

C. I consider my institution to be
   1. Urban (within city limits)
   2. Suburban (outside city limits)
   3. Rural (outside metro area) — C ______

D. My institution is
   1. Public
   2. Private
   3. Parochial — D ______

E. My institution is
   1. Coeducational
   2. All female
   3. All male — E ______

F. Using the scale provided below, please indicate what percentage of your population . . .
   1. 0–25%
   2. 26–50%
   3. 51–75%
   4. 76–100%
      i. Is white — Fi ______
      ii. Is black — Fii ______
      iii. Is Hispanic — Fiii ______
      iv. Is Asian — Fiv ______
      v. Is American Indian — Fv ______

G. Using the scale provided in question F, please indicate what percentage of your students reside on campus. — G ______

Please use the following scale to respond to all questions that request percentage information.

0 = 0–9%	4 = 40–49%	8 = 80–89%
1 = 10–19%	5 = 50–59%	9 = 90–100%
2 = 20–29%	6 = 60–69%	11 = Not applicable
3 = 30–39%	7 = 70–79%	12 = Unknown to me

Sexual Assault

(If precise figures are not available, please approximate.)

H. Of the on-campus sexual assaults reported to your office during academic year 1987–88, what was the:
   i. Number, excluding rapes Hi ______
   ii. Number of rapes Hii ______

I. What percentage of these sexual assaults were date/acquaintance rape? I ______

J. Of the on-campus reported incidents of sexual assault, what percentage . . .
   i. Resulted in criminal prosecution? Ji ______
   ii. Resulted in university penalty? Jii ______
   iii. Involved the use of alcohol? Jiii ______
   iv. Involved the use of drugs? Jiv ______

K. In your opinion, what percentage of on-campus sexual assaults are reported to campus police/security? K ______

L. What percentage of the above-mentioned incidents were perpetrated by nonstudents? L ______

M. Has your campus experienced an increase in sexual assaults during academic year 1987–88?
   1. Yes
   2. No
   3. Unknown to me M ______

Physical Assault

(If precise figures are not available, please approximate.)

N. How many on-campus physical assaults were reported to your office during academic year 1987–88? N ______

O. Of the on-campus reported incidents of physical assault, what percentage . . .
   i. Involved the use of deadly weapons? Oi ______
   ii. Resulted in criminal prosecution? Oii ______
   iii. Resulted in university penalty? Oiii ______
   iv. Involved the use of alcohol? Oiv ______
   v. Involved the use of drugs? Ov ______

P. In your opinion, what percentage of on-campus physical assaults are reported to police/security? P ______

Q. What percentage of the above-mentioned incidents were perpetrated by nonstudents? B ______

R. Has your campus experienced an increase in physical assaults during academic year 1987–88?

1. Yes
2. No
3. Unknown to me R ______

Vandalism

(If precise figures are not available, please approximate.)

S. Of the on-campus reported acts of vandalism that occurred during academic year 1987-88, what percentage . . .
   i. Resulted in property being damaged and subsequently repaired or replaced? Si ______
   ii. Resulted in criminal charges or prosecution? Sii ______
   iii. Resulted in university penalty? Siii ______
   iv. Involved the use of alcohol? Siv ______
   v. Involved the use of drugs? Sv ______

T. In your opinion, what percentage of on-campus vandalism is reported to campus police/security? T ______

U. What percentage of the above-mentioned incidents were perpetrated by nonstudents? U ______

V. Has you campus experienced an increase in incidents of vandalism during academic year 1987-88?
   1. Yes
   2. No
   3. Unknown to me V ______

General Information

Please use the following key to answer questions W-AA.

1. Yes
2. No
3. Unknown to me
4. Not applicable

W. Is your campus security force a sworn agent of or affiliated with a state or local police force? W ______

X. Does your institution have provisions for the immediate suspension of a student who constitutes a real or perceived danger to others on campus? X ______

Y. Is your office able to exercise the aforementioned authority? Y ______

Z. Do your feel that the majority of violent incidents on your campus are, in fact, reported? Z ______

AA. Does your institution have sufficient resources to control satisfactorily the impact of violence on your campus community? AA ______

Campus Violence Survey
Definitions

1. *Assault*—Any attempt to apply unlawfully the least actual force to another person. It is sufficient that there is an apparent intention to inflict a battery and an apparent ability to carry out such intention (aiming a blow, pointing a weapon, loaded or unloaded).

2. *Battery*—Any physical force or violence unlawfully applied to another person (may be committed by a jostling, tearing, or even touching of clothes worn).
3. *Sexual Assault*—Any intentional touching of any part of the victim's anal or genital area or other intimate parts for the purposes of sexual arousal or for the abuse of either party.
4. *Assault and Robbery*—By force or violence or by putting in fear, to steal and take from another person anything of value.
5. *Threat*—Any statement of intent to inflict future harm.
6. *Malicious Destruction of Property*—The willful and malicious destruction, injury, defacing, or molesting of any real or personal property of another.
7. *Rape*—Engaging in vaginal intercourse with another person by force or threat of force against the will and without the consent of the other person.

Index

D

E

F

G

H

I

J

K

L

M

N

T

U

V

W

Y

Z